# THE JUNGLE WAY

Keeping Your Teenagers Safe

Driving in the Asphalt Jungle

*Randy "Ra Ra" Rand*

by Randy "Ra Ra" Rand

and

Mark A. Werkema

Illustrated by Andrew Botting

THE JUNGLE WAY Publications.

ISBN # 978-0-615-64522-3

# TABLE OF CONTENTS

*- Alcohol, Drugs, Cellphone & Texting, Speed, Distraction*

# DEDICATION

To my wife and family, to all of the Jungle students, instructors and their families, and to every family who has ever lost a teenager in a driving accident.

**Randy Rand**

For Ashley and Chloe

**Mark A. Werkema**

Special thanks to my friends and family who have supported me in the arts, especially my mom. To everyone who has a positive dream. Dream big and keep humbly persevering.

**Andrew J. Botting**

# PREFACE

In an engaging and creative manner, the book *The Jungle Way* tells the story of teaching teenage drivers training from a unique, creative, and powerful method. Based on the business that Randy Rand created many years ago, the program was developed "to have as our primary goal to help save the lives of teenagers by teaching them the right way" and thereby reducing driving accidents. This book details that educational mindset and training process. The company that Randy started and created, training over 13,000 high school teenagers throughout the years, has proven to be an important model for effective teenage drivers training.

In this book of education and stories, the complete process and concept of *The Jungle Way* is detailed. What makes this program work, and how is it different from every other teenage driving program in the world? Jungle Survival Drivers Training is a corporation that meets the crucial goal to save the lives of teenagers by teaching proactive situational driving in practical and useful ways.

Teaching a teenager to drive is detailed in this book that focuses on training and skills that can last a lifetime as our teens "journey through the Jungle." This book also helps students and parents prepare for the challenging and demanding environment of the open road. In a new and innovative manner, *The Jungle Way* creates an environment where parent involvement is stressed, where student involvement includes preparation and focus, and where skill sets and thinking outside the box are the norm. The results are dramatic and effective. The driver's safety, essential to developing a cautious and proactive mindset for the safe teen driver, is stressed at every level throughout the program. "This is not drivers ed," says company founder and owner Randy Rand in his first meeting with every group of students and parents. "This is more about attitude, safety, and a mindset to teach students the right way to drive through the roads of the Jungle that lie ahead." *The Jungle Way* tells that story of how to accomplish those goals through an innovative, educational program. Open the door of your automobile, get in, buckle up, start the engine, and get prepared to take to the road safely with *The Jungle Way*.

# INTRODUCTION

What if I could convince you as a teenager, that safe driving skills to survive on the road are so valuable that you will most likely use them every day for the rest of your life when you drive an automobile? What if I told you as a parent, that helping your teenager to learn to drive safely and effectively would be one of the most valuable gifts you could ever give to your child? By learning these skills and reinforcing them to the teenage driver, a parent will have the confidence that their teenager will come home alive each time they drive a car. In essence, that is what this book is really all about.

My name is Randy Rand, and I founded a business called Jungle Survival Drivers Training which is dedicated to effective and safe teenage drivers training. This book is a desire to advance my message of our program further, and let more people know about our program and its benefits. If it promotes safety in the complex and often stressful process of a teenager learning to drive, then I believe it is worthwhile. But this book is intentionally written to teens and parents. Both play an important role in the process which we promote when a teenager learns to drive.

This book is entitled *The Jungle Way* because it has become such a creed of our business and what we believe in. This is our system that we have proven to be very effective and instrumental in teen lives. Simply stated, this book is an opportunity to help teach and encourage your teen driver to develop skills and become an established, safe driver. It is truly a gift that can last an entire lifetime, and be realized on every mile of road that they travel for the rest of their lives. Safe teenage drivers do not just "happen" – they have to be taught, developed, and instructed correctly. This book is all about doing that in an interesting and engaging manner.

First of all, let's get one thing straight. This is *not* a book about driving a Land Rover on a Safari through the Serengeti in Kenya, or somewhere in a remote game park in Africa, dressed in khaki shirts and pants with cameras at the ready to take pictures of the wild animals in the jungle. It's about the Jungle Survival Drivers Training system of driving, which I have developed, incorporating *The Jungle Way* where we teach teens to drive proactively. This is a unique program, different from anything else on the market, an "outside the box" way of thinking about what is commonly known as "drivers education", and it is the foundational goal of our company and the reason we are in business. There is a reason I picked the particular branding that would give someone that impression. Let me explain. It all has to do with the visualization and application. The system our company has developed perfectly matches the symbol of the jungle and the animals that roam within it.

# The JSDT Fleet

The Jungle Survival Drivers Training fleet is complete with nine different vehicles. Depicted here are seven of those vehicles. Each vehicle is painted to look as though they are morphing into a creature of the asphalt jungle.

## An Inside Look at JSDT

Here is what the Jungle Survival Drivers Training classroom looks like. The creative environment serves as a constant reminder that it is a jungle out there on the road.

It is how we teach our students to both approach and think about driving. It requires a very different methodology. Thinking differently about driving is what we are all about – and what makes us so very unique in our attitude toward safe drivers training. It is this unique style of thinking that sets Jungle apart from the rest.

I think most of you would agree that people learn more effectively by being able to visualize and then apply the training they have received. This is especially important with training teenagers because they have more of a "monkey see, monkey do" approach in learning how to drive. As a matter of fact, that's how most of us really learned how to drive and that is why we are all such *good* drivers! (Or, I should say, *think* we are good drivers.) I'll write more about the so-called *good driver syndrome* that prevents people from improving as drivers later in the book. *The Jungle Way* is simple, yet it only works if you apply it in your automobile every time you get behind the wheel to drive.

It is important to discuss what this book *is*, and what this book *is not* before we begin. First, it is not a "How-To Book", nor is it intended to be a book about facts, steps, or specific procedures. It is, however, a book about making teenagers safer and better drivers through attitude, mindset, and *The Jungle Way* of teaching drivers training.

Second, I won't give you lists, musts, or specific demands. What I will give you is a time-proven formula that saves teenagers' lives by making them better, safer drivers from the start. Lessons learned early on yield long-term positive results. We like to believe at Jungle that we teach them right the first time, which proves to be much more effective in the long run. Try this "system," as thousands of others have and you will come to believe by actually seeing the results, reaping the lifelong benefits and rewards of helping your teenage driver become a safer driver for a lifetime. (Remember, your teenager will soon be a young adult, a mother or father driving their children around town, and the automobile as a means of transportation will always be a major part of their lives.) Our company seeks to achieve this goal by a simple three-step process.

1. Improve and teach driving skills in an innovative and creative manner known as *The Jungle Way*.

2. This in turn reduces accidents and close calls by creating the right attitude.

3. This results in lowering the teen driving accident statistics. (by reducing accidents fatal and non-fatal, injuries, and deaths).

It is just that simple.

Finally, I have devoted my life's work and business endeavors to these worthy goals. I take them seriously – deadly serious, in fact, because I know all too well the price some teenagers pay in automobile accidents every year. These are staggering statistics and facts. According to a recent University study, 80 percent of teens will be involved in an accident during their first three to five years of driving, and 36 percent of teen deaths each year are a result of auto-related accidents. Over 5,000 teens die each

year in car accidents, 11 a day, and another 400,000 are seriously injured. Reducing high teen fatality rates has to be a priority of any drivers training program, and in ours, it is a cornerstone goal. Just one teenager death on the news or in a newspaper is one too many – our goal is to drastically lower the accident rates of teenage drivers, and Jungle strives to continually lower these saddening statistics. As I say to my Jungle parents, we don't want to have to go to your teenager's funeral. It is a sobering thought, but one that we would rather not envision. I want and need to get my message out and motivate parents and teenagers to embrace *The Jungle Way* as the only way to survive behind the wheel of an automobile.

Let's get back to *The Jungle Way* of driving. First of all, I would like to apologize to the real animals of the jungle for insulting them by comparing human beings and their driving styles and skills with jungle animals. In actuality, real jungle animals are more polite and courteous than human animals. Human animals in the asphalt Jungle are impatient, rude, angry, and overconfident regarding their driving skills. A great analogy, however, can be made between the automobiles and roads of the world with the animals and the Jungles in which they live. That is what we have created in *The Jungle Way*. The Rhino is one such example of Jungle vehicle animals.

# The Rhino

- The Rhino SUV is inspired by a rhinoceros, which teenagers would consider a cool SUV

- The mirrors are inspired by the ears of the rhino.

- The front vent is inspired by the rhino's nostrils.

- When comparing animals to vehicles, the wheels of a vehicle would be the feet of the animal which is why the rims of the Rhino have the toenail-like form in them.

- The sheet metal panels are layered similar to the armor of a rhinoceros.

*The Jungle Way* identifies driving styles and the type of vehicle driven with the real jungle animals. Chapter 1 contains a list of terms that we can visualize and use as an aspect of *The Jungle Way* of driving. As you may have noticed, the jungle out there is full of animals, and if you want to grasp the entire concept of *The Jungle Way*, we have to establish just what we are talking about with an understanding of the vocabulary and terminology used as part of *The Jungle Way* of driving.

I challenge you as teenagers and parents to read this book and learn the principles of Jungle Survival Drivers Training. Whatever you do, give it a try, and believe me when I tell you it will make you a better and safer driver in the long run – and remember, that is why we are in business. Our job comes with great purpose – to save teenage lives from behind the wheel of an automobile. Read on! Let's drive into the Jungle!

Randy Rand
Owner and Founder
Jungle Survival Drivers Training, LLC.
Ada, Michigan

# Chapter 1

## Jungle Terminology and Abbreviations

Let's begin with an explanation of the terms we use in Jungle. This is one aspect that makes Jungle unique – we use different terminology in describing other drivers and the vehicles they drive. On the surface you might think they are clever and amusing, but they really do all have a purpose and meaning. I have found that for the typical teenage driver, learning our way through the symbolism makes the program more intriguing, interesting, and engaging. Here are some samples of the way we "speak" at Jungle:

**Ants:** Ants are any pedestrians.

**Apes, Monkeys, and Chimps:** These are gawkers who stare at an accident scene, or something off the road. They point their fingers and think lots of things are funny. They are very nosey and are always trying to figure out how something happened or what's wrong, but they never do. As a result of their actions, they cause huge traffic jams by backing up traffic for miles.

**Bull Elephants:** Bull elephants are semi-trailers also called big rigs. They aren't about to move or get out of the way for anybody. They rule in the Asphalt Jungle, so don't anger them. Be respectful, be courteous, and stay out of their way.

**<u>Butt Sniffers & Butt Munchers:</u>** These are animals that follow way too close and do not drive *The Jungle Way*. The non-Jungle term is tailgating. Every Jungle driver knows that if you butt sniff you are likely to become a Butt Muncher (resulting in a rear end collision). The funny thing is you can't find a Jungle animal that will admit they butt sniff or tailgate because they all think they follow the animal in front of them with the right amount of distance. They really don't know what the correct safe distance is. The term "tailgating" originated, not from football games, but from horses in a herd, closely following the horse in front of them when they were in a stampede.

**The Big Cats:** (Tigers, Lions, Panthers, Cheetahs, and Leopards): The Big Cats are the best drivers on the road. They are very family-oriented, not unlike a family of lions (a pride). They are proactive situational drivers. They are stealth-like and very aware of everything going on around them at all times. They glide through the highway Jungle signaling properly, changing lanes properly, and executing complete stops while making right turns on red lights and at stop signs. They are always courteous and respect the rights of other animals in the highway Jungle. They are the only animals that possess The Four Characteristics of a Jungle Driver which we will discuss later. As a result, they never get taken by surprise.

**Alligators (Gators):** Gators are animals waiting to pull out into traffic from parking lots (swamps), side streets (paths), parking spaces (mud holes), and driveways. They can take you by surprise if you don't drive *The Jungle Way.*

**Elephants:**  Elephants are all large trucks other than semi-trailers.

**Gazelles:**  Gazelles are four-wheeled passenger cars that, just like the animal, are nimble and quick and travel in herds.

**Grhino:** This is a Rhino that's also a Gator waiting to pull out into traffic from a driveway, side-street (trail), or parking lot (swamp).

**<u>Ghippo:</u>** This is a Hippo that's also a Gator waiting to pull out into traffic from a driveway, side-street (trail), or parking lot (swamp).

**Hippos:** Hippos are older SUVs and Mini Vans which teenagers, usually females, think are uncool; most teens would never be caught driving one.

**Hyenas:** Hyenas are people who think they're good drivers when they're actually the worst on the road. They butt sniff all the other animals, but demonstrate road rage when others do it to them. They rudely cut people off, fail to use signals, and do just about everything else wrong. When other animals criticize them, they become extremely defensive. The best way to identify a Hyena is when they are complaining about another animal butt sniffing them. Just take a glance out the front window, and if there is an animal in front of them the Hyena will be butt sniffing them.

**Lemmings:** Most people drive like Lemmings. They react based entirely on the brake lights of the animals in front of them. They butt sniff so badly that they can't see beyond the animal in front of them, so whatever happens to the Lemming in front of them also happens to them. They'd follow another Lemming into an intersection (or off a cliff), and when a traffic light turns green, they go without looking.

**Mosquitoes:** Mosquitoes are bicycles that ride in the road and irritate the animals even though they have the same rights to the road as everyone else. They are very fragile and difficult to see. We must all be very careful around Mosquitoes.

**Piranhas:** Piranhas are motorcycles that glisten in the sun and quickly weave from lane to lane. They can sneak up on an unsuspecting animal and totally take them by surprise. Drivers must be very careful around them because they are smaller and sometimes difficult to see.

**Parrots:** Parrots are drivers who squawk and text on their cell phones while driving, and can cause a large number of accidents. In many cases, they are less aware of danger than an animal that has been drinking alcohol.

**Rhinos:** Rhinos are large SUV's like Hummers, Escalades, Denalis, or any other cool SUV with a cool status that a teenager would want to drive.

**Sidewinders:** Like snakes, drivers, weaving in and out, moving from lane to lane without signals or looking over their shoulder to check traffic, are Sidewinders. They speed without any concerns about the consequences.

**Swamp Rats:** Swamp Rats are rusted out, beaten up and dirty vehicles that look like they just crawled out of the swamp.

**<u>Tortoise:</u>** A Tortoise is a slow driver who is not aware of his or her surroundings. They don't pay attention nor are they alert. They drive in the passing lane 20 miles under the speed limit with their right turn signal on and won't move over for anyone. These animals especially anger Wild Dogs and Hyenas. When they are taken by surprise, which is often, they close their eyes, tuck their heads into their shell and hope for the best.

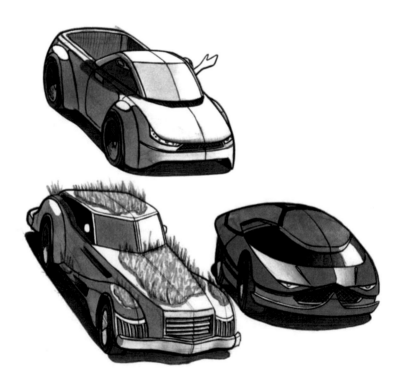

**Tree Sloth:** Tree Sloths live in the Amazonian rain forest, high in the trees and move so slow that they grow moss on their fur. Similar to older drivers, they have very slow reactions, drive methodically and think they are the only animals on the road.

**Wild Dogs:**   Wild Dogs are drivers who take a lot of chances, drive over the speed limit, roll through right turns on reds and stop signs, and don't care the least bit what the other animals on the road think.  They are so bold and over confident that they will admit they're bad drivers and are proud of all the things they do wrong.  There is not much hope for Wild Dogs.  Only skilled Jungle Trainers can tame a Wild Dog.

# WHAT IS JUNGLE REALLY ALL ABOUT?

Although this book is no substitute for attending one of drivers programs, some of the concepts will be discussed as we detail *The Jungle Way* to drive. There are two main documents which we hand to our students on Day 1 on a laminated sheet. These documents are *The Jungle Way Survival Methods* and *The Five Rules of Space and Visibility.* Each of these stresses the way which believe safe drivers should take to the road and approach the challenges of driving. Soon the safe skills become second nature among our students. This is our goal, and what we want to see in every student we train as they take to the road:

By developing these four characteristics into Jungle Way habits, a Jungle driver will never allow themselves to be taken by surprise.

## THE FOUR CHARACTERISTICS OF A JUNGLE DRIVER

1. Make your vehicle hard to hit.

2. Make the unexpected the expected.

3. Recognize doubtful situations.

4. Be aware of the uncertain actions of others.

# Chapter 2

## Attitude 101

This is a very important concept we teach: "The number one skill you can take with you when you get into an automobile to drive is having the right attitude." Driving with intelligence, skill, patience and courtesy is really about "attitude." Yes, this is a book about attitude. The only aspect of your life that you have complete control over, from the time you get up until to the time you go to sleep, is your attitude.

Sure, there are situations that occur during the course of an individual's day that impact their attitude, but an individual also chooses how to respond to those situations. Their response depends on a multitude of beliefs, perceptions, self-esteem, and their level of confidence, to name a few. As a human being however, the ability to decide how to respond rests with the individual.

Let me ask you, as a parent or a prospective teenage driver, a couple of questions which will set the stage. Why do I think that driver's training for today's teenager is so vitally important? Why do I believe it is a skill that will last a lifetime if learned correctly the first time? How does a teenager learn to drive in a way that is truly safe? Do you as a parent realize that what you and I can teach your child can save his or her life someday? That's right, you and I.

Without a high degree of parent involvement and mentoring, all the initial training teens receive will be wasted due to the negative external influences they will be constantly exposed to since the beginning of their driving career.

The Webster's Dictionary defines "attitude" as a "mental position with regard to a fact or state, a feeling or emotion toward a fact or state." That's a complicated way of saying mindset. And at Jungle, we preach mindset.

I believe attitude determines a lot of what we do in life. It has a dramatic influence on our daily life. And, not surprisingly, it does affect how we drive and the approach we take. In essence, *The Jungle Way* is about an attitude, a mindset. Hopefully this principle will become clearer over time throughout this book.

## SO, WHAT IS JUNGLE REALLY ALL ABOUT?

The way we learn to develop a proper attitude is through controlling three areas of space. First, we can control the space in front of our vehicle - we do this by creating the proper amount of space from the animal in front of us. Secondly, we control the space inside the vehicle - the environment. Thirdly, perhaps the most important space, which we can control - is the space inside our head - our attitude! As mentioned earlier, and it bears repeating, I teach my students from the time that they get up in the morning to the time that they go to bed at night; the only thing in life that they can control is *their attitude*. Jungle students learn how to take their positive attitude

41

with them into the vehicle and out into the jungle. After all, we are who we are and we drive based on our personality and attitude plays the number one role in preventing accidents.

Oh, by the way, you won't hear me speaking of Jungle and drivers education in the same breath during the reading of this book. It is my personal opinion the reason why auto accidents are the leading killer of teenagers in this country is due directly to drivers education and the format in which it is taught. I actually state to my parents in the parent training process that drivers education does not live up to expectations. In short, if not properly instructed, it can cost a teenager his or her life. In contrast, *The Jungle Way* saves people's lives. Drivers education does not work. Traditional drivers education fails to involve parents to the way that Jungle does. Since we began Jungle Survival Drivers Training, we have not lost a single Jungle student to a fatal or near fatal accident. Simply stated, our company is in business to make safer teen drivers and thereby save lives! My personal goal is simple – save just one teen life and it would be worth more than anything I had previously accomplished.

What should follow is the obvious. How is it being accomplished? Why is Jungle any different than any other driving school? What makes Jungle unique? Does it really work? Will *The Jungle Way* really keep my teenager safe and alive? Within the pages of *The Jungle Way*, these questions will be answered. Reading this book will amaze, entertain, instruct, motivate, and inspire you to know there is a proven and effective way to keep your most precious gift of life safe and alive in the highway Jungle. This is truly a unique and different approach to a teenager's educational experience and maturing – one they will take with them forever, through the rest of their lives, on every road upon which they will travel in future years. Parents, if you love and care about your teens, and I know you do, read this book and practice the principles daily with them.

As mentioned before, a book is not a substitute for attending one of our Jungle classes, but some of the concepts will be discussed as we detail *The Jungle Way* to drive. There are two main documents which we hand to our students on Day 1. The Jungle Survival Checklist and The Five Jungle Rules detail the methodology we use to train our students. Embedded in our methods are the four key characteristics of a Jungle driver that we instill in each student. Each of these stresses the way which Jungle believes safe drivers should take to the road and approach the challenges of driving. Soon, the safe skills become second nature among our students. This is our goal, and what we want to see in every student we train as they take to the road.

By developing these four characteristics into Jungle Way habits, a Jungle driver will never allow themselves to be taken by surprise.

Everything about Jungle is based on a proper attitude when we take to the road. I talk about this all the time in class. We stress it to all the teen drivers and their parents in everything we do. We want them to take the proper attitude with them every time they open the car door, get in, put the key in the ignition, start the car, and venture out into the asphalt jungle. Did you notice I said *every time*? That's what we preach...*every time.*

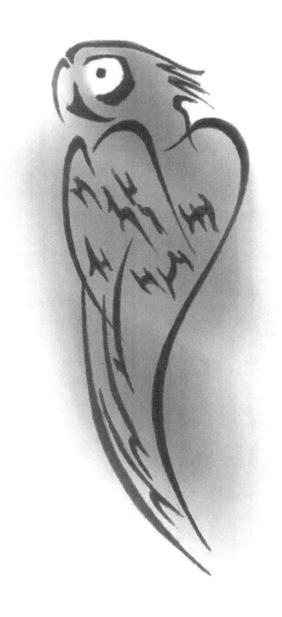

# Chapter 3

## It Can't Happen to Me

Everyone who writes a book has a reason and purpose in writing that book. For me, my purpose in writing this book was realized as a result of the circumstances of the following story.

There is an old saying in life that says, "It Can't Happen to Me." Certain stories have become legendary in the Jungle, and this is one of them. Younger siblings hear the lore and high tales of Jungle from their older brothers and sisters who have previously attended Jungle. This one story has become legend over time. Everybody wants to hear it told in their class when I work with the kids. It is an important story, not for its ironic and dramatic entertainment purposes, which the teens think it is – in fact, it is much more, because it holds a special place in my heart and it is a great teaching moment for the teens. The lesson and core premise of the story is crucial to understanding the asphalt jungle.

This old adage, "It Can't Happen to Me," the classic story of invincibility that all human beings are susceptible to in different endeavors – driving a car is no different. This story illustrates that yes, it can happen to anybody. It even involves me. I am here, gratefully, to tell you that truth in life.

It can happen to you as well.

Any day.

At any given moment.

This story involves me; herein lays the irony of this chapter. I'm writing a book about teen driving safety, and I am supposed to know what I'm talking about and have a certain level of expertise.

I'm not the best typist in the world; in fact, I might be the slowest. I'm even slower now because I only have nine-and-a-half fingers to type with as a result of one fateful morning while I was on my way to work. My left hand, even to this day, reminds me of the accident that nearly killed me. It is a day I shall never forget. Since this happened over ten years ago the actual physical pain is gone, but the mental pain is still with me, and it always will be.

After leaving a 24 year career at UPS and taking it easy for a couple of years, I realized retirement wasn't for me. And as a result, I accepted a position as Human Resource Director for a Native American community and their casino and resort in Michigan. I was fascinated by the opportunity to basically design and shape their Human Resource function and become involved with their culture and community.

The only drawback was the round-trip commute of 192 miles from my home to my desk at work. I decided early on that the distance I had to travel on a daily basis was worth the effort. This daily trek to work every day took its toll on my good driving habits that I had developed with UPS over the years. I was proud of my record and boasted about it over my career. One of the comments I use to make to all of my students in defensive driving skills was, "In twenty-five years of driving, the average driver will be involved in at least one auto accident, but *it will never happen to me because* I drive smart." As you will see, however, those words will come back to haunt me.

My new position was challenging, and the people I worked with were fantastic. One of the first challenges I had to address was the fact that even though the resort and casino had been operating for several years, there was a great need in many areas for a higher degree of organization and control. The tribe employed over 4,000 people, and there were very few rules in place to direct and hold their employees accountable.

Being the problem-solver type, I made the decision to form a team that would work to develop an associate handbook. The purpose of the handbook was to set standards for the associates and their managers to follow. Basically, it would be a rulebook.

After working diligently for several months, the handbook was completed. But, before it could be printed and distributed to the entire workforce, it needed to be approved by the Tribal Council. So, I scheduled a meeting with the Council for 8 A.M. on Monday morning. It was going to be a busy business day. I left for my daily drive to the reservation with a high level of energy and excitement. I couldn't wait to share the handbook with the Council and get the necessary votes, so I could get the book to the printers and distribute it to the workforce. The handbook was highly anticipated by the managers and supervisors. They felt it would give them the ability to improve their relationships with the associates and provide for better organization and accountability in the workplace.

My new job naturally involved a lot of driving in all seasons of the year and in all weather conditions. On this particular Monday, I decided to drive my daughter's Volkswagen Jetta on what was a rainy, dreary day. Gas had gone up to $3.50 a gallon, and the Jetta got about 39 miles per gallon. It took exactly one hour and forty minutes to get to my office. I decided to take a shortcut on one of the many rural roads. The casino was located in a rather rural area, and most of the roads were two-lane country roads with nothing but fields, trees, and farms on both sides of the road. There were deer everywhere!

Now, a few words of background on this story:

Even though I had spent most of my career at UPS involved in teaching just about every aspect of safe driving, I had been away from it for over three years and had started to develop a few bad habits. Due to the boredom of the daily commute, I would talk on my cell phone, drive a little too fast, and sometimes get a little sleepy. On this particular morning, I was traveling down a two-lane country road with scattered puddles of water everywhere. There were no shoulders on the road, so the road sloped off to the right and left down to an eight-foot drop.

Despite the bad weather, I was traveling at about 65 mph in a 55 mph speed zone when I decided to make a call on my handy, yellow Nextel phone. The pitfalls of stress at work were compounding in my thoughts and were a distraction while driving. I made this fateful call because I wanted to make sure that the tribal attorney talked directly to me. I had given the handbook to the tribal attorney on Friday. This was the person who said it would be no problem, and he was also the one who was on the handbook team the entire time it was being written. He was in approval of the handbook. I knew I would be asked by the Tribal Council if our attorney gave the book his blessings.

In order to dial the number I had to take my left hand off the steering wheel, so I was dialing while driving on a puddle-filled road, in the rain, at 10 mph over the speed limit. It was pretty stupid, to say the least. The attorney answered the phone on the first ring; it seemed like a good sign. I asked him, "Did you get a chance to review the handbook so I can tell the Council that you approved it?" His response was short and to the point. "No, I didn't and I don't think I ever will!" I responded with, "Are you serious? I'm meeting with the Council in thirty minutes to tell them the book is a go and has your approval!" The next words out of his mouth were beyond belief. He stated very calmly, "That's your problem," and he hung up.

I've been known to have a little bit of a temper from time to time, and this was one of those times. I was so angry that I threw the cell phone across the car and it struck the right passenger door. The next series of events happened in split seconds, but as I describe it, it seems like slow motion. This slow motion feeling is fairly normal for someone who is involved in an auto accident. This is the part of the story that became surreal. I can remember it as if it happened yesterday; that scene had been replayed in my mind thousands of times.

As I grabbed the steering wheel with my left hand, I couldn't believe my eyes. A deer was running toward the road from my left, and before I could blink he leaped from the yard below and on to the road, right in front of me. As he landed, he did a complete spread eagle and slipped on his stomach.

I always explain to my students, "You must never swerve to avoid hitting a deer, because, as a result you could go off the road and most likely roll your car over." I should have practiced what I had always preached. (Do as I say...not do as I did!) I swerved to my right, and at the same instant, hit my brakes. How stupid could I have been? I did the two things that a professional driver should never do. As a result of my temper and stupidity, my car hydroplaned.

I still remember the sounds, the eerie sounds of a car crash. Those sounds and that moment continue to haunt me to this day. As I stated before, this happened many years ago, the actual physical pain is gone, but the mental pain is still with me, and it always will be.

At this moment, all the skills that I teach to my students kicked into place. I got off the gas, counter-steered, and almost got the car under control. Instead of being a proactive driver, I was late in my response and my left rear tire went off the road into the mud. With the tremendous momentum and gravity, there was no way I could keep the car on the road.

As my car began to leave the road, I couldn't believe that "Randy Rand the Safety Man," as I was known as at UPS, was having his first serious accident. After training so many people for so many years, I was actually having an accident. I thought again about how I used to tell my trainees, "The average driver will have at least one serious accident in twenty-five to thirty years of driving. However, if you learn to drive the way I teach you, you won't be one of those people." Well, I became one of those people in a mere instant!

In a flash I knew I was in great trouble.

As the right corner of the front window began to crack, I remember the first roll over and that was it. What I remember seemed surreal, as if I was having a very bad dream. Suddenly, I felt this tremendous pain, more terrible than I had ever experienced before from any of my sports-related injuries. Those previous injuries included a broken ankle, a hyper-extended knee, and a broken nose. This new intense pain began at the top of my head and radiated throughout my body. Then suddenly, it stopped and I opened my eyes. Was I dead or alive?

It's difficult to accurately describe what I was thinking at this point. I was completely dazed, in shock, and embarrassed. After all, I was "Randy Rand the Safety Man," and I just had an auto accident! I couldn't believe this had happened to me; it had to be a bad dream. I wondered, "When am I going to wake up?"

As I sat in the car which had landed upright in someone's yard, I gazed out what use to be the front window. There was an eerie silence all around me. The morning sky was just beginning to show a little light. There was a wisp of smoke coming from the front of the car and all four doors were sprung open.

I was angry with myself. I took the distraction of my job with me into the car that morning…the trap that kills a lot of drivers on the road every year. I was, quite simply, not thinking about what I should have been concentrating on, and I paid the price.

I released my seatbelt and pushed open the driver side door which was barely hanging on by its hinges. I was dazed and confused. But, just before I got out of the car, I noticed I was astonishingly close to the side of a house and there was a lighted window that I gave a brief glance to as I stepped out of the car and stood up to survey the damage. My daughter's once-beautiful Jetta was demolished. Gone were the front hood and bumper, the trunk lid and rear bumper, and all four tires and wheels were flattened into the ground. It was an ugly crash, one that made my stomach turn.

As I emerged from the wreck I thought, "I'm not even hurt!" I began to walk around the car conducting an accident investigation; after all, that was my profession for so many years. As I was pacing off the various points of reference and the debris scattered across the yard, I heard voices from behind me exclaiming that I should sit down. I turned around and to my surprise there was an older man and a younger woman standing in front of me. They both had their mouths wide open with a look of amazement. As they were both imploring me to sit down, I noticed that they kept moving with a side-to-side motion. Almost as if I was throwing something at them and they were trying to avoid being hit. I found out later that they were dodging the blood that was shooting out of the end of my severed left index finger. As I waved my hands around in my attempt to explain to them what had just occurred, I was spraying blood everywhere.

The older gentleman ended up grabbing me and sat me down in my car. He explained to me that I was seriously injured and an ambulance was on its way to take me to the hospital. I kept telling him that I was fine and there was no need to call an ambulance. I know now that I was in shock, a delusional state of confusion. The next thing I knew a very bright light was blinding me. My first thought was that I must have died. You've heard the story of those who have near-death experiences report walking into the bright light in order to enter heaven. The other part of the story is you are supposed to be greeted by the people you knew who preceded you in death.

I was laying flat on my back staring into this light when I noticed several people standing over me. One of them had pretty bad breath. I thought, "People can't have bad breath in heaven." I started to feel around for my body. I noticed that I was still in one piece. I thought to myself, "Your body doesn't go to heaven with you".

Then things went dark.

The next thing I realized I was laying on a gurney and being lifted into an ambulance. I was also experiencing a rather pleasant floating sensation. I found out later that I was hooked up to an I.V., and morphine was being administered. To say the least, I wasn't feeling any pain.

Soon the side door on the ambulance was opened and a state trooper greeted me with, "Driving a little too fast for conditions, Mr. Rand?" I responded with, "Yes I was officer." I later received my very first ticket. It had been a wild day: my first ticket and my first accident.

As soon as the door closed behind the officer, the EMT, who was taking care of me, told me to stay calm and we would be at the hospital in about twenty minutes. He added, "We think you'll make it." My response was obvious: "What do you mean you *think* I'll make it?"

"Just stay calm Mr. Rand. Getting upset will only make things worse." I was calm and I wasn't upset due to the morphine coursing through my veins; it was the EMT who was panicking and creating a sense of fear in my mind.

Things went black again. I was out. It didn't matter because in the next instant I awoke in the hospital. I was laying in a bed in what seemed like a very large room. As I gazed around the room, I noticed that my pants and shirt were covered with blood. My left hand was in a metal dish filled with a red liquid, probably a disinfectant of some sort. I slowly lifted my hand from the dish, not knowing what I would see. It wasn't a pretty sight. My left index finger looked like an exploded cigar. Meat and skin hung down to the sides, and I could see the bone. I had lost about one-third of my finger. Most amazingly, I didn't feel any pain. I took my right hand and placed it around my exploded finger, squeezing it as hard as I could. My thought was to squeeze it so hard that it would form back to its original shape. As blood began to squirt out the top my cupped right hand, I decided this was a bad idea, so I put my hand back into the metal dish.

I felt as if I was dreaming and the whole experience was a bad nightmare. At that exact moment, I heard a squeaking noise followed by, "Mr. Rand, is there someone we should call to let them know of your situation?" As I opened my eyes, standing in front of me was a nurse who bore a striking resemblance to a chubby woodchuck standing on its hind legs with its front paws raised. I've always had the tendency to compare people to various animals. I don't know why; it's just the way I am I suppose. This had to be a dream; I was hallucinating. The morphine-induced haze and I.V. drugs in my bloodstream made the dream worse, but so vivid.

As she stood in front of me sniffing the air with her round button nose, I noticed she was holding my yellow Nextel phone in her right hand. She repeated, "Mr. Rand, is there someone you want me to call?" I responded, "Where did you find my phone?" She said, "It was given to the police by the homeowner, whose front yard your car landed in. It appears that he was in the barn behind the house cleaning out a couple of horse stalls when the phone came crashing through the wall of the barn and landed in the pile of hay, right in front of him. They figured it traveled over 200 feet in the air, over the roof of the house."

I asked Woodchuck Lady to please call my wife and my three managers who worked with me at the casino. She dialed my wife's work number and handed me the phone. I said the usual "hi" and she responded with, "Why is a nurse calling me and telling me you need to speak with me?" I replied with, "I had a car accident on my way to work; the car is totaled. I'm in the hospital and I lost the end of my finger. Want to see it?" I held my finger up to the phone, as if she could actually see it. She started to cry and hung up suddenly.

I must have passed out at this point, and when I awoke, I heard the words: "You look horrible. What happened to you?" I realized that this greeting was coming from one of my managers. All three of them were standing at the foot of my bed with a look of horror on their faces. After giving a quick explanation of my accident, as proof of my ordeal I held up my now shorter finger and asked them if they wanted to see it. This only added to their shock. "Put that thing away! It's disgusting," they said. I immediately put my hand back into the dish.

I must have passed out again because when I awoke, my managers had vanished. Standing before me was Woodchuck Lady. "There is a gentleman visitor here to see you and he said his name is Beaver," she announced. So here I was, lying in a hospital bed, covered with blood and glass, my index finger blown up, and a woodchuck telling me that a beaver was here to see me. This was definitely, a day to remember.

56

In reality, "Beaver" was what the Tribal Medicine Man was called. He was in charge of the tribe's cultural awareness and traditions. I told Woodchuck Lady he could come in to see me. As Beaver walked into the room, I noticed he was holding a supply of sage and cedar. The tribal members would use this combination to cleanse the area of negative spirits. After lighting the sage and cedar, they blow out the flame. The resulting smoke is spread around the room as specific chants are spoken to complete the cleansing ceremony.

Beaver came up to me and gave me a warm hug and asked for my permission to allow the Tribal Council to burn a fire in my honor at the Tribal Campground. It had never been done before for a non-tribal member and it was a great honor. Being the sentimental and emotional person that I am, I immediately began to cry along with Beaver.

As the smoke from the sage and cedar spread quickly around the room, my gaze shifted toward the ceiling at the sprinkler heads. My thoughts turned into prayers: "Please God, don't let the smoke set off the sprinkler system." I must have dozed off again because the squeaking of Woodchuck Lady's shoes on the tile floor awakened me. Beaver had vanished and all that was left was the smell of the smoke, which closely resembled the smell of marijuana.

As Woodchuck Lady entered the room, I awoke in fear. She stopped dead in her tracks; she looked around the room as if she was standing in a field sniffing the air with her button nose on her pudgy face. Her little paws up against her chest, and she was sniffing the air around her.

As she sniffed she said, "That Beaver man…was he… was he…smoking marijuana?" I didn't have the energy or desire to explain to Woodchuck Lady about Beaver's cleansing ritual, so I pretended to pass out. After checking my pulse to make sure I was alive, she squeaked out of the room.

Once more, I passed out and fell into unconsciousness.

Suddenly, I awoke to very unusual feeling in my left ear. It felt as if a piece of thread was being pulled through my ear. I could actually feel the vibration against the cartilage! I must have dozed off again because it startled me so much I sat up in bed. A voice with an unusual accent told me to lie back down and relax.

It was a doctor, and he was sewing up my left ear, which had been lacerated during the accident. He spoke with a very pronounced Indian accent, "Ear not look good, might lose ear, ear turn blue." I freaked out when he said that I might lose my ear. I said, "What do you mean ear not look good, might lose ear?" With a matter of fact response he said (again, with an accent), "Ear has turned blue, means there is lack of blood flow. If lack of circulation continues, have to amputate ear." My response was immediate. "No way, no way are you going to cut my ear off! I can't walk around with one ear; it would look horrible!" He said, "We replace ear with prosthetic ear. They look pretty good." I was emphatic. "I am not going through life with one ear! Call Betsy Ross, or somebody else, but start stitching Doc." When I realized he wasn't joking with me I exclaimed, "Listen, I play a lot of basketball. I can just see it now: I'm

driving for a layup and I get hacked in the head and my fake ear gets knocked off and slides across the floor. Instead of looking for a contact lens, everyone is trying to find my fake ear under the bleachers. No one would ever want me on their team. The ear stays on. Knock me out, sew it up, Doc, but whatever you do, I'll take my chances. The ear stays on!"

After laughing briefly, he continued to stitch up my ear. It took about nine stitches to complete the job. "All done," he said. He then informed me, "We have to take you down the hall to the CAT-scan room to take a look inside to make sure brain is okay."

Woodchuck Lady wheeled me down the hall, and at this point my wife was with me. As we were approaching the CAT-scan room, I told Woodchuck Lady that I loved her and asked her to marry me. She and my wife just laughed. I was obviously very appreciative of how well she was taking care of me. She laughed quietly and glanced at my medical charts to check just how much pain meds I had been prescribed.

As I entered the room, I was overwhelmed. The room was entirely encircled with French vanilla candles and my favorite song by The Eagles was playing: "Take It Easy." I couldn't believe it. How could anyone know that

French vanilla candles and this particular song were my favorites? It brought tears to my eyes.

Upon leaving the CAT-scan room, I thanked Woodchuck Lady for everything she had done; "Woodchuck Lady…" (I think this must have been the first time that I really called her this to her face.) She said "Pardon me!" I responded quickly with, "Nurse, thank you so much for the French vanilla candles and the music." She said, "What candles? What music?" I responded, "The French vanilla candles all around the room and my favorite song by the Eagles, "Take It Easy!" She told me, "Honey, there were no French vanilla candles in the CAT-scan room, we're not allowed to burn candles anywhere in the hospital. And there certainly wasn't any music in the room either." I was shocked because it seemed so real. I inquired, "Are you sure?" She replied, "Honey, I've got to get some of that stuff your on!" She shook her head, laughed, and walked away.

After the Eagles and candles, all I could think was, "What's next?" Almost on cue, Woodchuck Lady informed me that I would be taking a trip down to surgery to repair my finger. I asked her what they were going to do, and she told me that the doctor would explain that to me.

As if by magic, the next thing I knew I was lying on my back with my left arm outstretched through a white curtain on the left side of the bed. The curtain was high and wide enough so I couldn't see around or above it. Sitting in front of me on my right side was a very nice nurse who was applying a cold cloth to my forehead. In an apparent effort to keep me calm. She said, "Don't worry Mr. Rand. Just remain calm and everything will be okay." I wondered to myself: "Why is it that every time someone tells me to remain calm, something bad happens?"

As soon as the nurse told me to remain calm for the second or third time, I started to feel a poking and prodding sensation on my finger on the other side of the curtain. I could also hear what sounded like a large fingernail clipper or bolt cutter. It startled me because I couldn't see what was happening so I yelled out, "What's going on?!" Again the nurse implored me to remain calm.

Just as I opened my mouth to ask again what was happening, a doctor stuck his head out from behind the white wall and said, "Hi, I'm Doctor Johnson and I need you to remain very still while I try to make your finger look pretty."

"Look pretty," I said.

"Yes," he said, "I need to remove the nail bud from your finger. The nail bud grows your finger nail. If I don't remove it, when your finger heals, an ugly devil-nail will grow out the end of your finger." I asked, "A devil-nail, what's that"? He responded, "After your finger heals, a thick, ugly, orange and yellowish nail will grow out the end of your finger. Many times it grows to a point and you will have to file it down. It can be very painful."

A devil-nail doesn't sound like something that I would consider a positive addition to my now shorter left index finger. On the other hand, there are times during my classroom sessions it could come in handy when a particular student isn't paying attention. All I would have to do is point my ugly devil-nail at them and it might be just the ticket to getting them properly focused!

While the good doctor continued in his efforts to make my finger look pretty, I continued to ramble on about various thoughts running through my mind. I asked the doctor if I could have the part of my finger he was going to cut off. He laughed and asked why. I explained to him that I wanted to, maybe, have it gold plated and wear it as a necklace. He laughed again and explained to me that it was against hospital policy to give a patient their amputated body part. He could let me see it, but I couldn't keep it.

Although disappointed, I began to remember something to the effect that if I could locate the part of my finger that had been cut off in the accident, it could be reattached. It all started to come together in my sedated, drug-induced mind. Crows, the crow got my finger. That's the solution. Find the crow that had swooped down and grabbed my finger and the doctor could sew it back on.

As I lay on the operating table with my left arm outstretched, I began to make the sounds of a crow, quietly at first with just a faint whisper. As my excitement grew with the thought of reclaiming my finger from that rotten crow that flew with my finger in its beak, I began to caw louder and louder.

"Caw! !"

Can't you see it?

There he is flying over the hospital with my finger in his beak. Doc, we can catch him and get my finger back!

"Caw! Caw! Caw!"

At that exact moment, I heard a very loud clanging noise, as if someone had dropped a pan full of silverware on the floor. Everyone began to laugh hysterically and started to walk around the operating room. Scared and startled at first, I switched my focus immediately from the thought of catching the crow to the commotion that was taking place all around me. I yelled out, "What's happening? Why are you all laughing? What about my finger?"

As everyone began to calm down, the doctor looked at me from around the curtain and said, "Mr. Rand, in twenty years of cutting people's appendages off, I have never heard anything so hilarious as the thought of a crow flying over this operating room with one of those appendages, specifically, your finger in its beak. I'm very sorry if we scared you. I hope you realize that there isn't a crow with your finger flying over us." Sadly, I realized he was right and with my hopes dashed, my thoughts shifted to how I could get even with every last one of those rotten crows and those useless deer. After all, they were the cause of my current predicament!

I knew a long time before the accident that I didn't like crows and deer. The morphine-induced dreams continued. The crows bothered me because they were sneaky. How can they swoop down onto a road or highway and eat dead animals and never get sick or die? How come they never get run over as they stand, picking away at a carcass and fly away at the last split second as a car approaches? Everyone knows that crows are the symbol of death....just ask Edgar Allen Poe. They freak me out. Every time I see one I get chills and think about the surgery table and morphine hallucinations.

On a funny note, I see my experience also as a metaphor for "eating crow" and making some bad mistakes in life on the road. Yes, I had to eat crow here. I was embarrassed and humiliated. Everyone at UPS who found out about this wanted to see my finger and talk about how it could happen to "Randy Rand the Safety Man" at UPS.

Let's not forget our friend, the deer...the bane of driving accidents. I like wildlife, but deer have become a major problem on American roads. Here is a fact from the Michigan State Police: Over 650 people die each year in America from deer-automobile accidents. Other than for hunting and making me crazy, they serve no useful purpose on this earth...I would love to line the fields and ditches along our highways with salt blocks to attract the deer. Once they approached the salt to take a lick, I would mow them down with an Uzi machine gun. This is a simple but effective solution to ending deer-automobile accidents and saving 650 innocent motorists every year! Pardon the sarcasm, with all due respect to the ASPCA and PETA, but I think of the 650 funerals and the families' grief that cannot be forgotten. In truth, the biggest lesson I learned was that I let distractions affect my driving, and the result was disastrous.

After my surgery, I was transferred back to my room. I was greeted with a concerned but happy family. A short time later I was released from the hospital and I was wheeled down to the lobby. To my surprise, I was greeted by a chauffer; he was proudly standing in front of the tribal limousine. I was whisked away to the top floor of the hotel. The tribe was very gracious to my family and me. They insisted that my family and I stay in the Governor's Suite located on the top floor of the hotel. We spent two days there so I could recover. At the time there was a rumor floating around the reservation that I had lost my left arm, had a fractured skull, was going to die in the Governor's Suite, and be buried at the Tribal Campground. To say the least, I had a good laugh over it.

After making a complete recovery, minus a little bit of my finger, I returned to my normal responsibilities. Life returned to normal until one uneventful day. I was sitting in my office when a young man approached my door and asked if he could speak with me. He introduced himself and explained to me that he was a Table Games Dealer in the casino. He was a very pleasant young man in his early thirties. We talked for a few minutes, and after getting to know each other a little bit, he abruptly changed his focus and demeanor. He said, "I wanted to talk with you in person in order to make you aware of something that you might want to know."

I looked at him with a newfound interest and said asked, "What is it that you want to talk to me about?" He said, "You know the place you where you had your car accident?" "Yes I do," I replied. "After you rolled your car, well, that was my front yard you ended up in. The old man and the young lady that helped you were my father and my wife," he said.

I told him I was very grateful to them for all of their help. He said something next that was beyond belief and affects me to this day.

He continued, "Do you remember seeing a lighted window and the side of a house when you stepped out of your car?" I nodded yes and wondered what he was trying to tell me. He said, "That lighted window was my kitchen window."

He paused.

"The side of the house you said you noticed was the wall of my kitchen".

He shook his head.

"You are probably aware that your car rolled at least five times." I told him I was aware of that fact. He continued and said, "Are you also aware that if you would have rolled one more time you would have crashed through the wall of my kitchen?" This I know – I should have died, my neck snapped, broken bones, or a head injury for certain.

I suddenly became speechless and he continued without waiting for my response. He said, "You know, my wife saw your car as it was flipping over. She was at the kitchen sink putting diapers on my four month old daughter. You see, she had just given her a bath in the sink and when she heard the crash, she looked up just as you landed upright after your last flip. If you would have rolled over one more time you would have probably killed my wife and daughter and maybe yourself."

It's hard to accurately explain my feelings at that exact moment. I was shocked, stunned, saddened, and grateful all at the same time. He quietly stood up and walked over to me and I also stood. He hugged me and said, "God and all of His angels were watching over you and my family. He saved you, my wife, and daughter for something greater." He thanked me for listening and talking with him and walked out of my office as quietly as he walked in. It was a big break, and I received a gift...a second chance. I knew I had to tell others this story. I knew I had to incorporate this lesson into the curriculum at Jungle someday because it was such a valuable lesson.

My accident happened over ten years ago, and I use the memories as a constant reminder to me of how different my life would be if I had caused the death of that young mother and her daughter. I will always be eternally grateful to God for sparing the three of us and there isn't a day that goes by that I don't thank Him. I took with me that day the lessons of invincibility, over-confidence, and pride. I learned something from an accident that could have very well taken my life, and it was one of those difficult and painful lessons.

The simple, but profound, valuable lesson that morning was this: It *can* happen to anyone, including me. It can happen to any teenager who takes to the road, any parent, or ANY driver. I have a constant reminder of that day and the hospital dreams...my left hand and the smaller index finger that carries with it a story which I shall never forget.

# Chapter 4

## The Sad Statistics

The facts about teenagers and driving are startling. The statistics, unfortunately, do not lie. Here are a few facts that you as parents and teenage drivers should know.

In a recent University study it was found that 80% of all teenagers will be involved in some sort of auto accident in their first one to three years of driving. In their first year of driving at the age of sixteen, one out of seven will be involved in a serious accident. Most alarmingly, each year 36% of all teenagers who die in the United States will die as a result of an auto accident.

There is hope for our young drivers. That is exactly why we teach what we do. As part of *The Jungle Way* of driving, we conduct surveys on an ongoing basis to determine if we are as effective as we think we are and how we can continuously improve in our efforts to keep these young people alive. I have always believed in continuous improvement in everything I do, because if you don't think you can improve you never will. I also say, if you don't get better you will get worse.

As a result of our Jungle surveys, we have found that only 10% of Jungle students will experience an auto accident in their first one to three years of driving. Although a tremendous improvement over the reported

80%, I think we can do a great deal better with more parent training and involvement. This is important to realize because previous studies and our own experience training over 13,000 teenagers have demonstrated that no matter what we teach at Jungle, our students will ultimately drive like their parents, good or bad.

As stated earlier, my intention in writing this book is not to overwhelm you with statistics and charts showing how many teenagers are dying, but rather what we *can do* to learn driving the right way the first time a teenager learns to drive in the impressionable, early years. One of our Jungle mottos is, "It takes thirty days to form a habit and thirty days to save a life." We have a very short window of opportunity to get what we want into the heads of these young drivers. Think of it this way: when they come to Jungle to be "Jungalized" we just get them crawling. By the time they leave they are starting to walk and it's up to the parents to keep them walking by continuing the "Jungalization" process during the first thirty days they drive with their teenager. Our goal is to effectively motivate and inspire the parents and their teens to drive *The Jungle Way* for life.

This book is my philosophy on driving all wrapped up into one simple, yet entertaining read. What you can learn from this book, you will be able to take with you for a lifetime. I am confident that by reading this book and applying the principles of *The Jungle Way*™ of driving for thirty days, you will become *jungalized* and as a result you will drive with the right attitude and a higher level of skill and awareness.

It's all up to you.

# Chapter 5

## The Design Process

**Illustrator's Notes**
**by Andrew J. Botting**

# The Bull Elephant

The Bull Elephant is similar to the Elephant in that the grill is inspired by the wrinkles of the elephant's trunk, and that the tire tread is inspired by the nails on the elephant's toes. The large rear view mirrors of the truck represent the large ears of an elephant. I know truck drivers often enjoy customizing their rides, so I felt the need to add pin striping to the truck. The pin striping design resembles an elephant.

# The Elephant

The Elephant is a large truck with a grill detail that is inspired by the wrinkles that are formed on the trunk of an elephant. The large rear view mirrors are a little extra large just as the ears of an elephant span out so greatly. The tread on the wheels of the Elephant are inspired by the toenails of the animal because the wheels of a vehicle would be the equivalent of the legs on a animal.

# The Gator

The Gator was a lot of fun. It has a green paint scheme to match the color of the alligator. The side air vents are formed to match the wavy shape created by the animal's mouth. With aggressive headlights, and a sporty, aggressive stance, the car captures the eagerness Gators have to catch you by surprise and jump out into the road. The air vents on the hood are inspired by the rugged armor of the alligator's skin. I couldn't resist adding the plate that reads "L8TER" for the phrase "Later gator".

# The Gazelle

The Gazelle has prominent ventilation on its hood. Those vents are inspired by the antlers of the gazelle. The gazelle's face is captured in the front end of the Gazelle vehicle. The headlights are the eyes, the secondary turn signal lights are the ears and the smaller vent in the middle of the car is inspired by the nose of the gazelle. A graphic detail runs through the side of the car to match the stripe on the animal. The car's antenna was inspired by the tail of the gazelle.

# The Lemming

The lemming is a small critter, so I felt it necessary to make the Lemming a small, smart car sized vehicle. The eagerness they have to just drive and follow other drivers without questions asked is captured in the face of the vehicle with a grill wide open as though its smiling. The graphic on the vehicle is inspired by the fur marks on the lemmings.

# The Mosquito

The Mosquito bikes seemed to be a great match with the mosquito insect. The fragile, thin legs of the insect provided a great opportunity to use as inspiration for the bicycle's frame. The aggressive stance of the mosquito was incorporated into the bicycle's stance as the frame leans forward. The spots on the insect's body became graphic details on the bicycles.

# The Parrot

The Parrot is a customized, tuned sports car with a body kit. Having a rally, or GT style sports car with some bells and whistles was the best vehicle choice for the Parrot to be able to have a brilliant paint scheme that matches the parrot's feathers.

# The Piranha

The Piranha has a glossy, metal flake paint scheme to resemble the sparkle a piranha fish has. The framework, motor details, suspension, rims and brake calipers are a vibrant orange just as the piranha fish has an orange belly. The background of the motorcycle sketch is blue to symbolize tropical water.

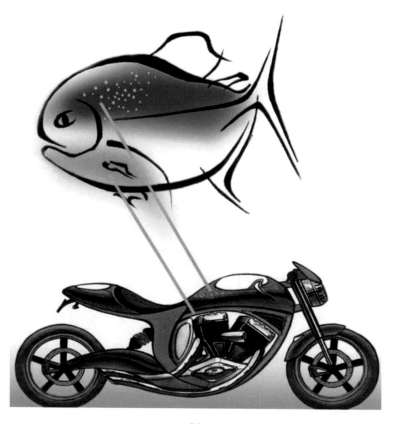

# The Rhino

The Rhino vehicle has layered sheet metal panels just as a rhinoceros has armored skin that appears layered. I felt that the wheels of a vehicle are like the animal's legs, so that is why the rims of the Rhino have the semi-circular form in it to look like the toenails of a rhino. The vehicle's logo emblem is a horn and the light directly behind it poses as the second horn. The rear view mirrors on the Rhino are inspired by the ears on the rhinoceros. The vent in the bumper was inspired by the rhinoceros' nostrils. The vehicle's shadow clearly depicts its roots...the rhino.

# The Sidewinder

The Sidewinder motorcycle is inspired by a snake. The wavy form of the snake is incorporated in the form of the bike as the diagram below shows. The fang of the snake is resembled on the bike by the fang-like air vent. The rear vents were inspired by the belly of the snake. The bike's logo on the gas tank is in the form of an eye. The rear of the motorcycle is inspired by the back of a cobra.

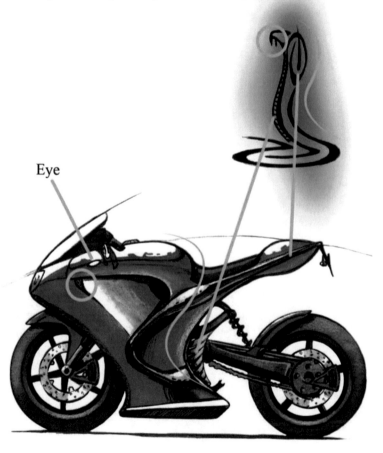

Eye

# The Swamp Rat

The Swamp Rat's sheet metal tells a story. The Swamp Rat has a lot of hours logged on the road. As the rust shows, it has seen its fair share of rainy days. This Swamp Rat was in a small accident which damaged its hood and bumper. The mismatching rims add a little bit of character to the Swamp Rat. This vehicle may not be as flashy as some other cars out there, but it definitely has what it takes to keep trucking on the road.

# The Tiger

The Tiger has an orange paint scheme, which when the lighting is right, it also shows white reflections in the glossy, polished paint. The white reflections resemble the white stripes of a tiger. The step, bumper, trim, and rims have black paint as they are inspired by the black stripes on the tiger. The seal around the headlights resemble the black fur around the eyes of a tiger. The lighting inset in the front bumper was inspired by the gums of the tiger.

# The Tree Sloth

The Tree Sloth vehicle has fenders that are inspired by the long arms of a sloth. Since the Tree Sloth drivers are often drivers from an earlier generation, I wanted to hold on to the vintage car feel and incorporate large, rounded fenders. The turn signal lights are inspired by the sloth's claws. I'm excited about the floating headlight element that allows air to flow underneath it.

# Chapter 6

## Reasons

I wrote this book for teenage drivers and their parents. I had been thinking about writing a book regarding this topic for many years, and with the development of *The Jungle Way* of driving, it was finally time to put pen to paper and write this book. Many have asked me to explain my reasons for writing this book. I want to explain why I believe so much in Jungle. This book explains our creed and beliefs at Jungle, but it also explains why we are in business. Many of you might ask, "Why write a book about a subject that is considered boring and has already been written about numerous times? What makes your book, your system, and your concepts different?" These are the questions which I want to explain. It is the heart of how to understand *The Jungle Way* from start to finish, and helps to develop a greater understanding of what our goals are and why we have established them.

I've spent a good part of my life helping people to be safe. My first non-paying job was in fifth grade as a school crossing guard, and boy, was I proud when I was promoted to a crossing guard captain and traded in my silver badge for a gold one. I loved that job. I had my yellow helmet, white crossing belt, and my gold badge; I couldn't have asked for more. I took that job and my responsibilities very serious, and at such a young age it never occurred to me that I had taken the first step toward my destiny.

I'm sure you have heard the philosophy that all of us are put on this earth by God for a specific reason. We all have a purpose for being here. Many of us never discover what our true purpose is for being here. We never know at what point in our life that knowledge will be revealed or mistakenly discovered. Some of us are never fortunate enough to figure it out, because finding your life's purpose is elusive. I was one of the fortunate ones, and my reason for being was revealed when I was given that gold badge. Helping people, plain and simple, is what I'm here for.

It sounds great, doesn't it? To help people, take care of people, and put other people's needs before your own. I think that's what being unselfish is about. There are many ways to help others and it's not as easy as it sounds. Some people don't think they need help, others don't want help, and some just don't trust others enough. Some people even believe when help is offered it's because the person doing the offering is really only looking to get something in exchange.

Practically speaking, however, how do I teach these young drivers my philosophy? How do I make a lasting impact on them in a short time that will affect their lives forever? Some simple steps I have developed over the years have greatly helped. An explanation is in order.

I always explain to my Jungle students my simple philosophy of life: spend your time collecting people not things. Always put the needs of others before your own and help them achieve their goals, aspirations, and dreams. Let them know, by your deeds, that you have a sincere interest in helping them in any way you can, and they will follow you to the ends of the earth. If, at the end of your existence in this world, you can count at least five friends that would do anything you ask if needed, then you can consider yourself a successful human being.

Many Jungle students are confused and wonder what my philosophy has to do with learning how to drive a car. They came to Jungle to learn how to drive so they could get their permit and begin their travel down the road of independence from their parents, or so they think.

Writing a book is a challenging task. I had to ask myself, what did I hope to accomplish and would anyone pick it up off a shelf and read it? Would it make a difference, and would it help to provide solutions to the tragedies, that occur all too frequently, for many families across our country? So, let me begin by answering my first thought as to why.

Teenagers are dying at an alarming rate due to poor driving - to a dance, to a football game, to a movie, to a party, or just joy-riding with friends. It's happening all too frequently, and every time a teenager is killed, injured, or causes harm to someone else in an auto collision, everyone seems to helplessly accept the tragedy and move on with the hope that it won't happen again. The majority of these deaths and injuries *can* be prevented with the proper training and guidance.

I know full well that I'm not the only one who cares about the safety of teenagers. Obviously parents care for and love their children and want them to be safe. There are many people who work in the teenage driving industry who also care about the safety and well being of these young drivers. As a matter of fact, teen driving fatalities and injuries have been reduced significantly in many states due to the efforts of many of these people. There is a lot of good work being done and significant progress is being made, but unfortunately, it's still not enough.

While I was formulating the concept of Jungle Survival Drivers Training in my mind, I immediately thought it would be a great idea to investigate how other driving schools taught teenagers how to drive. I thought perhaps I could learn something from them. After all, we are all reaching for the same goal. We are all doing everything in our power to teach young people how to survive in the highway jungle.

I spent a great deal of time visiting various drivers education schools in the area I lived as well as in the surrounding communities. It was an interesting experience to say the least. I immediately noticed that my background was significantly different than the people who were running and teaching these various drivers education programs. Most of them were current or former school teachers, retired police officers, or people who just wanted to own their own business, or supplement their income. I'm quite sure that all of them feel as though they are doing the best job they can to teach teenagers the right way to drive a car. Many of them would most likely consider themselves experts in the field of drivers education.

After visiting these numerous schools, I realized there had to be a better way to teach teens to drive – a safer way, more effective, more engaging, more committed, and particularly one that had a greater impact. I developed *The Jungle Way* to preach my doctrines and principles of driving safely and proactively. I wanted to impart my philosophy to my students, and their parents, so that when they enter into the highway Jungle they are equipped properly and ready to face what awaits them.

# Chapter 7

## "I Don't Throw Up Anymore When I Drive with My Teenager!"

Strange title for a chapter of a book, don't you think? If you are reading this book however, you were curious enough to pick it up and begin reading at least the first page. But it's not as strange as you think. There is a meaning woven into this chapter. It's actually a statement made by a parent of one of my students who I was helping to prepare for their road test with the road test examiner. There is actually meaning behind what she said.

This is another story that has become quite legendary in the Jungle. We prepare young people for the challenges of the highway Jungle; in short, we teach them how to survive amongst the wild animals they will encounter in this Jungle.

Let me tell you a brief story of how interesting and wrong perceptions of drivers training can be from people who approach the topic.

As part of our lifetime commitment to all of our Jungle graduates, we encourage them to return when they are eligible to take their road test in order to practice and be evaluated. The first thing I ask the parent who brings them to the session is, "Can you take a nap while you are in the car when your teenager is driving?" If you can see the look on the parent's face when I ask the question, it's priceless. At first they laugh nervously and think I'm just joking with them. When they realize that I'm serious, they give me this look of amazement and laugh again. A few, and I mean a very few of them, reply with, "Of course I can. My son (or daughter) is an excellent driver."

On one particular day I asked one of my mothers this same question. She was a rather tall and imposing woman, easily six feet tall. When I asked her my usual question, she gave me this incredulous look and said to me, "Are you kidding me? You can't be serious!" I responded with my usual explanation. "You know, you are shortly going to be making the decision to let your teenage son drive your car by himself. He is going to be driving a three- to four-thousand pound missile down the road with every type of wild animal driver out to get him. Don't you think you should be completely confident of his driving capabilities at this point to know for sure that he will return home safe and sound?" At this point, she looked down at me and I realized that she had to be at least six feet, two inches tall because I'm almost six feet, and for a brief moment I thought she was going to hit me. Thankfully she just smiled at me and said, "Can I take a nap when I'm driving with my son? Can I take a nap when I'm sitting in the passenger seat while my son is driving me down the road? Honey, not only can I not take a nap, but just a week ago I quit throwing up when I drive with him!" At this exact moment her son looked up at her with an exasperated expression on his face and said, "Mom, you only threw up that one time!" I laughed so hard I thought *I was* going to throw up!

The world of Jungle Survival Drivers Training is filled with stories like this one. After all, everyone has a pre-conceived image of what drivers training is all about. This image is obviously based on a parent's own experience when they took drivers education at their perspective school as a teenager.

# Chapter 8

## "Dear Parents, a Letter You Must Read"

I write this letter to the parents, spoken directly from the heart. Parents play the most vital role in the teen driving process. Teen driving studies and our own firsthand experience has shown that teens will drive like their parents, whether that be good or bad. This will occur in spite of the quality of training they receive in drivers training. I always laugh when people tell me that I must have nerves of steel to teach teenagers how to drive. The reason I laugh is it's not the teenagers that worry me; it's their parents.

I like to say in Jungle, "The parents are the wild animals, they give us their offspring, we tame them and train them, then we give them back to the parents – and the parents have the potential, at least, to make them wild again." It's a funny, but also a sad comment because in many cases, the parents actually undo what we so painstakingly create in the time we spend with their teen.

I know you love your son or daughter more than anything in this world. I also realize you would do anything to keep them safe and out of harm's way. You definitely don't want some stranger telling you how to raise and take care of your children. But the facts don't lie. Uninvolved, overconfident, poorly trained, and "I'm-a-good-driver" parental mentality are the primary reasons auto accidents are the leading killer of teenagers in this country. Strong statement, I'm sure you would agree, but true.

Many parents can say, "Everything I ever learned about driving that was bad I learned from my dad." This is typical, and the "old school" driving instructor at the local high school wasn't much better. Parents somehow think they can effectively teach their children to drive by taking them out to the church parking lot and tell them the finer points of driving in one afternoon. There could be nothing further from the truth. Think of the character Kevin Arnold in "The Wonder Years" television show and his overbearing, yelling dad teaching him how to drive. Sometimes, father does not know best, unfortunately. The sad thing is that many parents think this is a completely normal way of teaching drivers education. This is all too commonplace, but not really effective.

Out of frustration, I will repeat what I previously stated: *You are the wild animals, and you give us your offspring to tame and train and then we return them to you, and you make them wild again!* It's a never-ending struggle that literally makes me want to scream, which I have done on several occasions.

I have an idea for a second book – its title would be: "CRASH COURSE IN DRIVING: Why You As Parents Need to Re-Learn Driving the Correct Way, Even If You Think You Know It All." Well, you might find the title a little offensive or you might object to it, but just consider for a moment what you as a parent might learn from your teenager during this course. I know some parents might not believe me, but if they

read this book in full, they too will become better and safer drivers.

Are you talking about me?!

I hope to dispel the myths and legends of "Old Way" (drivers education) verses "New Way" (*The Jungle Way*™) of learning to drive. The Jungle Way™ is somewhat unconventional, but if you as a parent give The Jungle Way™ a chance with your teenager, I am confident you will see positive and dramatic results. I know this to be true because all of the parents who have previously sent their teenagers through Jungle make the same comment: "It's amazing how much better my son/daughter drives compared to my older children who weren't able to attend Jungle because you weren't in business at the time."

Dismissing the "Old Way" is not an easy task with many parents due to their perception of what drivers education is all about. Their perception is based on their own experience when they were teenagers and they took drivers education through their school. Their instructor was usually one of their teachers or a coach. Although well meaning, many of these teachers never received the high level of training which is required to inspire teenagers to drive to survive. Just think back on your own drivers education training; do you even remember the name of the person who taught you and what you actually learned? I'll help you out: You learned to keep your hands at ten and two o'clock on the steering wheel and to maintain a following distance from the vehicle in front of you equal to one car length for every 10 mph. Let me guess...I'll bet most of you don't do either of these two things. Don't worry; neither one of them are the correct methods even though they were taught and still are in many drivers education programs across the country.

The effort of dismissing the "Old Way" of drivers education, which I like to term an "unlearning drivers education," is a difficult task. Sometimes old habits die hard, and new ways are hard to grasp. But, I can assure you this: if you embrace *The Jungle Way* with your teenager, I guarantee that you will learn skills that you did not previously know about survival driving and the principles of how to survive in the highway Jungle.

Let me explain and share with you a couple of short stories that will bring greater understanding to my philosophy regarding parents and their impact on the survivability of their teenage driver in the highway Jungle.

# "Dad, You Didn't Stop!"

The other day in class I was asking my usual questions of my students. For example, since you've been in Jungle I'm sure you have been paying more attention to how your parents drive and more specifically, how they drive in comparison to the way you are being taught. Could you please raise your hand if you've mentioned to your parents what they are doing differently to what you've been taught in Jungle? Usually, pretty much everyone in the class raises their hand with enthusiasm. I then go around the room and ask them to share with the class their experiences.

One young lady said that she notices that her dad doesn't stop completely when he's making a right turn at a red light, nor does he stop completely at stop signs.

"I pointed out to him that at Jungle they teach us that a complete stop is always accompanied with a slight bounce back, and then you know you've made a complete stop," she stated.

I asked her what he said in response and she said with a smile on her face, "He told me he doesn't stop because he is trying to conserve fuel." Obviously, the class broke out in laughter.

I hear contradictions from parents all the time. Amazingly, parents claim knowledge and experience in what they consider to be "the real way to drive." What we teach in *The Jungle Way* is often compromised and dismissed by the parents if they do not become part of the active process and embrace *The Jungle Way*. That's why it is so important to have them involved in *The Jungle Way* Parent Training, which we include in our curriculum and require all parents to attend, which will be explained later in this book.

In another class, I was with a student and it was his first day on the road. Actually, it was the first time he had ever been behind the wheel of a vehicle. As we were approaching a stop sign at a very busy and dangerous highway with speeds of approaching traffic well over 55 mph, I noticed that the young man was not moving his right foot to the brake from the accelerator pedal. I immediately applied my secondary brake and stopped the car at the stop sign. I asked him if he was planning on stopping and his response was unusual to say the least. "My mom said it's not necessary to stop completely." I looked at him with amazement, thinking he was joking, so I laughed a little and so did he. It didn't take me but an instant to realize that he wasn't joking.

I immediately, with quite a bit of, let's say feeling (because I never yell at my students), explained to him the importance of complete stops and his responsibility to protect the side of the car, which is the weakest part of the car. I went on to reiterate that 10,000 people die every year at intersections due to side impact collisions.

His response was incredible. "My mother showed me how to run both stop signs *The Jungle Way* and it's safe."

I said, "How can running a stop sign with cars coming at you from the west and then crossing a divided

highway and running a second stop sign with traffic coming from the east at 55 mph, or more, be safe?"

"My mother showed me and it really works. As you are approaching the first stop sign, you look left at the oncoming traffic, and if it's clear you look to the right at the second stop sign. If it's clear in that direction, then you accelerate through both stop signs. She said she does it all the time and with practice I can become very good at it also."

I was amazed, to say the least. I asked him, "What makes her such an expert at driving skills and running stop signs '*The Jungle Way*'?" (By the way, I never teach running stop signs *The Jungle Way* or any other way!)

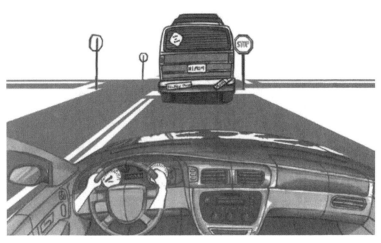

**Wait for the bounce back while stopping.**

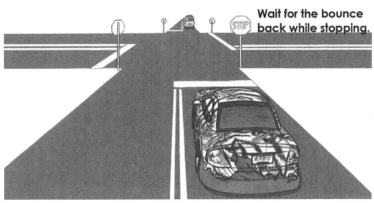

**Drive!**

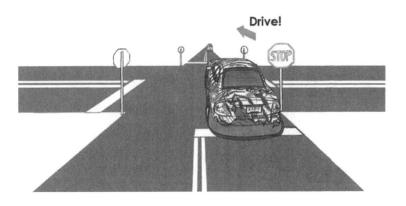

He said, "My mom is in sales and she drives 5,000 miles a month, so she has a lot of experience and practice. She also has never had an accident or received a ticket in her whole life."

With driving credentials like his mother's, how could I convince him that she was wrong without making her look like an idiot to him? I made a point to speak with her as she came to pick him up after his drive time. As she drove up near where I was standing, I walked up to her and shared my experience and the incredible explanation of how to run a stop sign which her son had shared with me. I thought for sure he was making it up. What responsible parent would teach their teenager to do something so incredibly unsafe and illegal, and then wrongly associate it with the techniques we teach at Jungle?

When I shared with her what had happened on her son's first day driving at his very first stop at a stop sign, she said "Yes, I did demonstrate the running of stop signs to him, but I would never want him to attempt such a maneuver without the right supervision and practice." Remember what I said about parents making me want to scream? Well, this was one of those times! It's a hard story to believe, but entirely true.

I have had numerous discussions with parents and teens regarding the inconsistent follow-up training provided by parents while driving with their teenagers. When teenagers graduate from Jungle they obviously are not a finished product. Their level of knowledge regarding *The Jungle Way* of driving is excellent, but they lack the behind-the-wheel driving experience. It is vitally important for them to learn how to apply what they learned at Jungle. I always tell the parents that "Jungle teaches them to take their first steps into the highway Jungle, but you are the ones who you teach them to walk."

Most every state or drivers training expert is of the opinion that behind-the-wheel driving experience is the most important aspect of insuring that teens learn to drive the right way. I wholeheartedly agree with this philosophy. As a result, parents are responsible for making sure that their teenager gets plenty of practice driving a car with either or both parents acting as their drivers training instructor.

Unfortunately, this is a plan for failure. This failure is one of the primary reasons why auto accidents are the leading killer of teenagers in our country. It's much like the old saying that "the blind are leading the blind." Parents teaching their teens how to drive to survive are like a coach who doesn't know the plays and has never even played the sport they are attempting to coach. I'm not saying that parents aren't capable of teaching their teens how to drive. It's just that I don't think they are properly equipped to do a quality job. If given the right training and tools to get the job done, many of them would do an outstanding job of teaching their teen to drive correctly.

When a parent has a teen that struggles with a particular subject in school and the subject is beyond the parent's educational level, they recommend that their teen get extra help from their teacher. If they can afford to, they hire a tutor. If a teenager wants to learn to play a musical instrument, they learn through their school's music teacher, and if the parent can afford it, they take private lessons. If their teenager wants to play a sport, they try out for a team at school and they learn how to play the sport and its fundamentals from their coaches. In all of these examples of teenage learning experiences, the parents understand in most cases that they don't have the knowledge, or skill level to assume all of the various teaching roles.

When it comes to driving a vehicle, most parents feel they know enough about driving that they can surely teach their teenager how to drive correctly. After all, they've been driving for years, their parents taught them everything they knew, and besides, it's not rocket science! The, "I know everything" attitude or the "been there, done that" mentality many parents posses is another root cause of the unacceptable teenage crash rates. This attitude exists despite the fact that they themselves were never properly trained and their driving expertise was learned over the years by observing all of the other wild animals in the asphalt Jungle drive the wrong way. The majority of their driving skills were acquired through simple old-fashioned trial and error. In many of those situations where people learned through trial and error, they never survived the error!

I know for a fact that many parents would most likely not send their teenager to a drivers training school if the state they lived in didn't require it. It would be a relief for them not to have to pay, and they honestly feel that they could effectively teach their teen how to drive better anyway. This feeling is founded on their low opinion of the drivers education industry based on their own personal drivers education experience. This mentality has contributed to what I call the "Good Driver Syndrome."

## "The Good Driver Syndrome

## and the Church Parking Lot"

I know parents mean well most of the time, but when it comes to driving, sometimes fathers and mothers do not know best. Let me explain as I outline the problem.

Whenever parents decide to allow their teenager to enroll in a driver training program, they believe it is better to take their son, or daughter out prior to the class to give them a little practice training so they will know what to do. They learned this philosophy from their parents, and their parents probably learned from their parents. It's a generational thing. This task is usually a father's responsibility unless it is a single parent household, then the mother becomes the brave soul who ventures out into the church parking lot with their excited, but nervous, teenager. I know, usually, no real harm is done other than it's against the law, but it can cause a major attitudinal problem. Here's why: it's the beginning of what I call the "Good Driver Syndrome." This is when the entire false perception of "I'm a good driver" attitude actually begins.

Let me explain. When a teenager is learning how to drive, their first emotions are of fear, apprehension, or nervousness. They need support and encouragement to overcome their feelings. This support and encouragement is obviously provided by the loving mother or father who ventures out to the church parking lot with their new fledgling driver.

The normal church parking lot training session lasts as long as it takes the parent to get bored or scared, usually about twenty minutes or less. The parent first teaches the teen about how the controls inside the car work, followed by a few laps around the parking lot. The parent typically focuses their efforts on the skills they struggled with when they were first learning how to drive. During and at the end of this intense training session, the parent will offer words of support and encouragement regardless of how their teen performed. Statements like, "You did a good job," "I'm very impressed," "You're a natural," "With more practice you'll make a good driver," and "We didn't even come close to hitting a light pole." I don't think that any parent would tell their child they were horrible and they must be insane for letting them take drivers training, or they almost took out every pole in the parking lot and it was a good thing God was watching over us!

In some cases, teens have gained previous experience while learning to drive an ATV, lawn mower, golf cart, go-cart, or maybe they grew up on a farm and were taught to drive a variety of farm equipment. Many teenagers growing up on farms gained their first experience sitting diaper-clad on their father's or grandfather's lap while they were plowing a field. They find the church parking lot experience rather easy and even a little boring. Their main focus is getting their license and getting out onto the road.

As a result of their previous driving experiences and the encouragement they received along the way, the "Good Driver Syndrome" was firmly cemented in the minds of these young beginning drivers forever. They might have a few setbacks along the way as they continue to learn to drive. Their first time in heavy traffic someone might cut them off, or a Gator might pull out in front of them. They might have a difficult time making turns, or centering their car in the traffic lane without going off-roading. Sometimes, a simple properly executed lane change can be a very difficult maneuver that shakes their confidence until they master it. Their first time on the expressway entrance ramp accelerating up to 70 mph is always a beginning driver milestone. Getting off the expressway can be equally challenging not only for the new driver, but also for the Jungle trainer.

The following story will demonstrate what I mean about the shaken confidence of a student and the instructor. I shall never forget it, and it perfectly illustrates my point.

# "Oh My God! We're Going to Die!"

Okay, time for another legendary Jungle story, and this one is a classic!

It was a beautiful summer day, not a cloud in the sky, a great day to venture out onto the interstate in the *Beast* (a fourteen-passenger, three-ton van) with my students to teach the art of entering and exiting the express-way. You know, the acceleration lane and the deceleration lane! We use the Beast to enable our students to experience the unique handling characteristics and capabilities of different vehicles. Many of them will be driving larger vehicles, and parents appreciate the fact that we can provide the experience and practice.

On this day, I decided to take three students out onto the expressway in the Beast. Driving the Beast was Steven, and in the seat right behind Steven on the left was Daniel, who in three weeks of class never spoke a word; he just sat in the back of the room with his armed folded across his chest. Another student named Claire was sitting behind me on the right side of the Beast. I was sitting in the right front seat, close to my trusty secondary brake. My students were all equally nervous, and maybe frightened. Steven, due to the fact that he was the driver, was nervous to be venturing onto the expressway for the first time; Dan and Claire were nervous because they were passengers in a vehicle that Steven was driving.

Steve was a very unique teenager.  First of all, he was a very large young man of fifteen.  I would estimate that he was about six feet, four inches and weighed over 250 pounds.  In addition, Steve had an unusually high-pitched voice being prepubescent.  He looked much older, and I had to constantly remind myself he was only fifteen.  Due to the fact he had grown so fast at a very young age, Steve was rather clumsy and uncoordinated.  I don't say this to be demeaning, but I want you to imagine the situation I was about to experience.

One aspect of *The Jungle Way*™ of driving is we teach our students how to verbalize what they are thinking and seeing while they are driving.  Part of this training involves the Jungle Trainers acting as Jungle guides by verbally explaining the Jungle methods while the student is driving.  This approach firmly cements in their minds what they have studied in class along with the practical application of the Jungle methods while they are behind the wheel.  The following is an actual account of what I affectionately refer to as the "Oh My God!  We're Going to Die!" story.

"Okay, Steve.  We are now entering the entrance ramp 96.  We curve around back to the right, the acceleration lane begins, and we are going to accelerate up to the speed limit which is 70 mph.  The acceleration lane will eventually become the right lane of the expressway, which will have a total of three lanes.  Once we have merged on to the expressway, we are going to change lanes into the center lane because on a three-lane expressway the center lane is the lane of least resistance due to the two upcoming entrance ramps on our right.

110

"Give it some gas and put your left turn signal on, not the right one, Steve. Left, down is left. Up ahead to the left, do you see the two wider white lines that come together to form a point? That is the weave lane, and we are not allowed to cross over those lines. We will move over when the dashed white lines begin. Okay, this is similar to a lane change. Our left signal is already on, so continue to accelerate. As we pick up speed, glance into the rear view mirror and quickly checking our left driver side mirror; without moving your shoulders, just your head, glance 90 degrees to your left to double check alongside the car. Even though we have the mirrors adjusted *The Jungle Way*, I still want you to use your eyes as much as possible.

"Continue to accelerate as we move into the center lane because we want to blend with the other animals that are on the expressway at the speed they are already traveling. This is called driving with the flow of traffic.

Most animals are driving at 5 to 15 mph over the speed limit, so if you are driving too slowly you can possibly become a hazard. With all the distractions inside the other cars, it doesn't take much for someone to look away for a brief moment and there you are in front of them going 20 mph under the speed limit.

"Excellent transition into the center lane! Good job! Up ahead to your right there are two entrance ramps where other animals are merging on to the expressway. Even though you have the legal right of way, we want to be courteous and let the merging animals get onto the expressway. We have three ways to let them on. We can move into the left lane to create a gap for them, or we can slow down or speed up to let them in. We'll just stay in our lane and let up on the gas so they can fit in front of us. We will do the same thing right up ahead at the next entrance ramp.

"Steve, an interstate highway actually crosses over various state borders; hence the reason it's called an interstate highway." (At this point I usually go into a detailed visual explanation of the specifics of the Interstate Highway System. Steve couldn't have handled it...)

"Steve, we're going to head on down the expressway, and we are going to get off at Exit 36, which is the Leonard Street exit. You see the solid white line on the pavement to our right? When that line becomes a broken or dashed white line, that indicates the beginning of the deceleration lane which is when we want to begin slowing the Beast down. Just before that point we are going to signal and perform our center mirror check, right mirror check, and then check with our eyes to the right. Remember, don't move your shoulders when you glance or it will move the steering wheel and that could be dangerous. Also, don't stare over your shoulder; just a glance is all we need. If you stare, the vehicle will move to our right and we would be forced over the white line and onto the shoulder. If that should happen, you will feel the rumble strips, which you can see, along the right edge of our lane.

"Okay, Steve. You can see up ahead the large green sign which indicates that the

ahead of us. Remember, we have to check our mirrors every five to eight seconds, and as we look into our mirror we have two Gazelles butt sniffing us really bad. Just lightly tap your brakes a couple of times and we can get them to back off of us a little. The exit is coming up and the sign tells us that the exit ramp speed is 25 mph. Signal right, check your center mirror, right side mirror, and check over your shoulder to the right."

The next part of the story is more effectively told with an explanation. I say this because if any of you have seen your life pass before your eyes or experienced a near death experience, this was my version of such an experience.

In his high-pitched voice Steve began the process of moving over into the deceleration lane. "Signal, mirror, mirror, shoulder," squeaked Steve. He glanced a little too long over his shoulder, and as he did the Beast moved over the

The rumble strips make a very loud noise in the Beast due to the higher tire inflation level, and this took Steve by surprise. It must have scared him because the next series of events scared all of us who shared in the experience. Steve decided to steer the Beast hard to the left away from the rumble strips. At this point the Beast, for a fraction of a second, shuddered as it fought to stay upright. I immediately grabbed the steering wheel to straighten the beast out. Suddenly, Steve decided he was going to hit the brakes, but instead of applying the brakes, he nailed the accelerator to the floor with his huge right foot. As the Beast roared ahead toward the exit ramp and the rapidly approaching 25 mph curve, Steve took his hands off the steering wheel, covered his eyes and all I heard was Steve yelling at the top of his voice, "Oh my God! We're going to die! Oh my God! We're going to die!"

While all of this was happening, I heard sounds coming from the back seat, where Dan was sitting and he was screaming so loud that if there was a glass in the Beast, the pitch of his voice would have broken it.

So here I was, Steve, with his gigantic leg and foot holding the accelerator to the floor, his hands covering his eyes while he was yelling, "Oh my God! We're going to die!" While Daniel in the back was trying to shatter glass with his screams; don't forget Claire. I can only imagine what was going through her mind. Then there was me! I acted instinctively and hit my good old trusty secondary brake to slow the raging Beast down. Although I managed to partially slow it down, it was still moving forward at too high of a speed. I had only one choice. While holding the wheel with my left hand to keep the Beast straight. I reached over with my right hand and punched Steve on his right calf. I had no other choice, and it worked! He quickly pulled his foot off the accelerator pedal and yelled at me that I hurt his leg. So, between "Oh my God! We're going to die!", "You hurt my leg," and Daniel still screaming in the back seat, I was able to regain control of the Beast and slow it down as we approached the exit ramp.

As we reached the stop sign at Leonard Street and I stopped the Beast, Steve finally took his hands off his eyes and remarked, "Oh my God! We didn't die!" Despite all of my years of teaching people how to drive to survive, I had to admit, I almost wet my pants!

As I looked over at Steve, I noticed the two Gazelles that were following us pulled alongside of us. They were laughing hysterically!

Little did they know that if we had flipped over in the Beast, since they were Butt Sniffing us, they would have become part of the resulting accident.

After I calmed down and composed myself, I said to Steve in the calmest voice I could muster, "Steve why did you swerve and push the accelerator down? You could have killed all of us." His response was expected. "I got scared and I thought I was applying the brake." "Why did you take your hands off the wheel and cover your eyes?" "I thought I was going to crash and I didn't want to see it."

I then looked in the back seat at Daniel and Claire. I asked Claire if she was alright and she responded with nervous smile that she was okay. I then looked over at Daniel and said, "Daniel, was that you screaming like a little girl?" With his usual blank look and unemotional voice, he spoke for the first time in three weeks. "Maay bee…" The resulting laughter in the Beast rapidly eased the tension, and we continued on with our training ride.

The expressway driving adventure for the beginning driver can be an eye-opening experience. Just the thought of going on the expressway can invoke fear and apprehension in the minds of young teenage drivers. It never fails, even though we review expressway driving in class, as they are approaching the entrance ramp they will always ask what the speed limit is. I always respond with "In most states the maximum speed is 70 mph and that's the speed we will be accelerating up to." In many cases, their response is, "I thought it was 75 mph!" I already know the answer, but I ask anyway. "Where did you learn that?" As expected, they reply, "From my parents. They told me you can go 5 mph over and the police won't catch you!"

Parents, I would like to give you some good advice. Please take it to heart. I hope you realize that you are not perfect drivers, and many of you aren't even good drivers! But, you have to understand something. You are your children's real role model when it comes to most things in life. This also holds true for the way you drive. As I have stated earlier, your children will ultimately emulate what you do behind the wheel, good or bad. Just remember, like father like son, like mother like daughter.

Sometimes, regardless of what we tell them, students learning *The Jungle Way* of driving tend to be more critical of other drivers. When they observe you doing something wrong, or unsafe behind the wheel, don't get upset. Definitely refrain from defending what they caught you doing wrong. Use that moment as an opportunity to evaluate your child's level of understanding of what they learned in Jungle by asking them questions about the wrong action and how it could be improved.

This positive interaction is especially important during the first several times you drive with your new teenage driver. We have a motto at Jungle "Thirty days to form a habit, thirty days to save a life!"

Make it a personal goal and set the right example for your teen. I always explain to my students that speeding is speeding and the so-called 5 mph rule that many people use when they drive is an excuse used by speeders who travel 10 to 15 mph over the speed limit. When they see a police car they slow down to 5 mph over. At that point if they aren't pulled over by the police, they usually speed up again when the police are out of sight. I always like to ask them if they've ever witnessed their parents doing this and they usually respond with "All the time."

My students always inform me that their parents told them that you can go 5 mph over and they won't catch you. Remember that 70 mph is an intimidating speed for most beginning drivers. This fear of expressway driving also carries over to the parents when they are presented with the opportunity to share in the adventure with their new driver, fresh out of Jungle.

The "Good Driver Syndrome" attitude, developed at such a young age, makes almost everyone who drives sensitive when anyone critiques their driving, even by the people who love and care about them. I always say, "Never be critical of three things: a person's religious beliefs, their political beliefs, or their driving skills."

This "Good Driver Syndrome" also prevents driving improvement. After all, how can you become a better driver when you don't have the motivation or desire to improve because you're already of the opinion that you're such a good driver?

I know for a fact that everyone who drives has been criticized about their driving. I'm sure at some point it's happened to you and probably more than once. When you were critiqued, did you enjoy it? Did you sincerely thank the person who pointed out your flaws? I'll bet you told them that you will do everything in your power to take their suggestions and practice them every time you drive and just hope and pray you can live up to their expectations. Maybe the next time they drive with you they will tell you how much you have improved and they feel much safer. I don't think so!

Most everyone who drives thinks they are a good driver. They feel it's their right to point out other driver's bad driving habits and lack of skills. However, they never say anything negative about their own driving skills and habits. This is a good time to refer to the Jungle Terminology listing I provided you with because what I just described is a Hyena!

Parents teach many lifelong skills to their children, and one of these skills is how to drive safely in a challenging environment for a lifetime, which is bound to change over time as the years pass. As the parent of three children myself, I know the value of teaching something to your kids that is lasting – and driving the right way is a gift we can give our children if we are actively involved in the process. The truth of the matter is this: the children whose parents are actively involved in the process are much better and safer drivers in the end. We all need to work together to keep our future generations out of harm's way in the asphalt Jungle. Parents play a key role in that equation! It is just that simple. Remember this, as it can't be emphasized enough.

Helping your children to be happy and safe should be a primary goal of any parent, so let's get serious about it. We need to work closely together to accomplish this goal. I think it's ludicrous and absolutely unacceptable that 36% of our future is being needlessly killed on our nation's highways. Enough is enough! It doesn't have to happen and I have proven this. *The Jungle Way* is a drastically more effective way to motivate, inspire, sell, and ultimately teach the teenage driver how to "drive to survive." We can and have improved road safety and accident rates. We just need to learn and follow *The Jungle Way* of driving so we can continue the development of better and safer teenage drivers from the start. This is my life endeavor, my creed, and my motivation.

Parents, please help me accomplish this by helping your children learn to drive in a manner that will promote these necessary and worthwhile safety goals.

# Chapter 9

## "The Expert and the Parent"

There are many different places that you can learn to drive in today's world. That really scares me, because a certain claim is often made. Who are "the experts" in drivers training today? We are all experts, right? The word "expert" is often tossed around in the company's advertising and brochures. Just look what is out there to teach your kids to drive. There are school systems that teach driving as an elective course. (Parents, think of your high school days and the math or social studies teacher doubled as a driver's education teacher after school.) This is actually a serious problem with respect to the parent's attitude toward drivers training. This is the point in time where everything goes wrong and one of the primary reasons why auto accidents are the leading killer of teenagers.

When it comes to teaching a teenager how to drive, the worst-case scenario is a teen being taught by a parent who thinks they know what they are doing when they don't. I don't say this as a form of insult toward parents and their efforts to keep their kids safe. I am a parent also and I care deeply about the happiness and safety of my kids. But, a parent without the proper training and support can actually contribute to the endangerment of their teen when they are finally allowed to drive by themselves.

Let me break this down in simple terms so I'm not misunderstood. I was watching TV the other day and a commercial came on that began with a customer in a cell phone store asking the salesperson question after question about the capabilities of the cell phone. The commercial then went to a doctor's office where his doctor was examining the same individual. After the doctor had completed the examination he asked the patient if he had any questions regarding his exam. With a blank uninterested look on his face, the same guy asking all of the questions at the cell phone store had no questions for the doctor.

The same attitude exists with many parents when it comes to their teen taking drivers training. I honestly believe that if many states didn't require drivers training as part of the state law for teen licensing, parents wouldn't pay a dime for their teen to be properly trained, especially when they think they are fully capable of training their child.

This attitude exists due to a couple of reasons. One reason is the parent's perception of drivers training based on their own experiences when they took drivers-ed as part of their school's program. Let's face it. Traditional drivers education is not highly regarded as an effective form of training in most people's minds. Most people who took drivers education can't even remember the name of the teacher or coach who attempted to teach them nor what they were taught.

Secondly, driving a car is all about the lines, signs, markings, laws, and how to maneuver a car through traffic without their teen hitting anything, or scaring them. If you asked most people, "Are you a good driver?" most would answer with a resounding, "Yes!" I always laugh when someone tells me they are a good driver because I know it isn't true in most cases.

Many people who claim to be good drivers base this claim on how many tickets or accidents they have had. Although any driver should be proud if they have never had either in their driving career, it doesn't necessarily make them a good driver. The real question they should ask themselves is how many close calls or near misses they have had in their driving career. Do they properly signal all lane changes and do they even know what a proper lane change is? Do they make complete stops at all stop signs and right turns on red lights? Do they drive faster than the posted speed limit? Do they think a green light means to go? Have they ever gotten mad at other drivers? Have they ever had a drink of alcohol and driven a car? Do they talk or text on their cell phone? Do they always wear their seat belt and make sure everyone in their vehicle wears theirs?

I could go on and on with this type of questioning. The point I'm making is that none of us is a good driver. We can all improve, and we all do things behind the wheel we shouldn't do, but we do it because we are human beings who are capable of poor judgment and the resulting mistakes we make when we operate a motor vehicle.

Parents can be their own worst enemy when it comes to how safely and alert their teen drives. Parents set the example for their young drivers from the first time they put them in that infant car seat in the back of the car. As their teen becomes older and watches how their parents drive more closely, their training truly begins. The old "Monkey see monkey do" adage is now in effect.

When people find out what I do for a living the usual reaction is one of three things: I'm crazy, the most patient person in the world, or that I have a death wish. They would never do what I do. But the truth is, it's not the teenagers that drive me crazy. Teaching them *The Jungle Way*™ is easy. They think it's cool to drive *The Jungle Way*™. It's the parents who drive me crazy.

People think that simply because they have been driving for many years they know how to drive properly. This belief couldn't be more untrue. When you are first taught a task, how do you become good at that task? First off, your initial training has to be based on sound methods and principals. Second, a trained professional should administer the training with proven results in their area of expertise. The trained professional's training should be of the highest quality with required follow-up training as needs and technology change. The results achieved by this trained professional should be monitored, recorded, and measured. This expert trainer should be evaluated on a regular basis to determine their level of effectiveness in order to hold them accountable for the results they achieve. This person should be required to develop closely monitored and realistic goals. They should not be a person who provides the training as a part-time trainer to supplement the pay they receive for their regular full-time occupation. Third, this trained professional should have documented experience in all areas of their field of expertise.

What I am describing is pretty standard for just about any job where someone is in a training position, with the exception of a drivers education instructor. Imagine that...teaching teenagers how to do the most dangerous task they will ever be required to do...drive a car. Being taught by someone whose only claim is they have done it for a long time and therefore have years of experience which must make them an expert is not enough!

How many teens have they trained who have had auto accidents and as a result were killed or crippled, and if not killed, they are hooked up to life support in some medical care facility? Or maybe they were unharmed and they killed or crippled someone else due to their poor training provided by their drivers education instructor and their parent's feeble and unskilled efforts to train them and hold them accountable for driving the right way when they themselves don't even know the right way. These explanations are the leading causes of teenage deaths in our country. It begins with a never-ending cycle of improperly trained, or never trained instructors who consider themselves experts, training teenagers who learn nothing, who grow up driving a car with the misconception that they are good drivers based on driving the same wrong and dangerous way as every other driver on the street.

This is why I have a disdain for someone who considers himself or herself an expert. What is an expert anyway? An expert would refer to an individual who has worked in their chosen field for a significant period of time while achieving a degree of success or level of excellence. It seems like every time I have met or worked with an individual who was labeled as an expert, I was disappointed. It seems as if the label itself prevents a person from getting better at what they do. After all, how can you get better when you are already an expert?

There are many former and current experts across the country who taught or who are teaching teenagers how to essentially drive a three- to four-thousand pound missile down the road without killing themselves, their passengers,

or other drivers. But, how effective have all of these experts been? The answer is simple. Even the experts themselves agree that teaching teenagers how to drive the correct way is almost an impossible task.

## Practical Parent Tips

# FACTORS SHOWN TO BE IMPLICATED IN TEEN DRIVING ACCIDENTS

- **No. 1—Driver inexperience**. Crash rates are highest during the first year a teen has a license. Provide as much supervised driving practice as possible—at least 50 hours or more over a period of no less than six months. This will help your teen gain the skill he or she needs. Even when your teen has a full license, it is a good idea to limit his or her driving during risky conditions. These include driving at night, in bad weather, on highways, and with teen passengers. Allow more driving privileges as your teen gains experience and skill.


- **No. 2—Driving with teen passengers.** Crash risk goes up when teens drive with other teens in the car. Nearly two out of three teen crash deaths that involve sixteen-year-old drivers happen when a new driver has one or more teen passengers. Follow your state's Graduated Drivers License laws for passenger restrictions. If your state does not have a teen passenger rule, you set the law – no friends in the car for at least the first six months when your teen is *driving* on a restricted license. Then make sure your teen doesn't *ride* with another teen driver who is driving on their restricted license in the first six months.

- **No. 3—Nighttime driving**. Nighttime fatal crash rates for sixteen-year-olds are nearly twice as high as daytime rates. Nighttime driving is risky because it is harder to see at night and people are often tired. Be sure your teen is off the road by 9 or 10 P.M. Stick by this rule for at least the first six months of your teen having his or her license.

- **No. 4—Not using seat belts.** In 2007, six out of ten teen drivers and two out of three teen passengers who died in car crashes were not wearing seat belts. The simplest way to prevent motor vehicle crash deaths is to buckle up. Wearing a seat belt will cut your teen's risk of dying or being badly injured in a crash by about half. Remind your teen to wear a seat belt on every trip—even just for a drive around the corner, and teen drivers need to make sure that the car doesn't move until all the passengers are buckled up!

- **No. 5—Distracted driving.** Nearly eight out of ten crashes happen within three seconds of a driver becoming distracted. Common distractions for teen drivers are talking on cell phones, using in-car electronic devices, text messaging, eating, playing with CDs or the radio, and yelling out the window. Forbid all activities that could affect your teen's driving attention.

- **No. 6—Drowsy driving.** Young drivers are at the highest risk for drowsy driving, which causes thousands of crashes every year. Other than late at night, teens are most tired and at risk when driving between 6 to 8 am, and from 2 to 5 pm after school. Be sure your teen is fully rested before he or she gets behind the wheel. Make sure they go to bed at a reasonable time before school if driving.

- **No. 7—Reckless driving.** Research shows that teens lack the judgment and maturity to assess risky situations. Help your teen to avoid the following unsafe behaviors:
  - **Speeding.** Make sure your teen knows to follow the speed limit and adjust speed to road conditions.
  - **Butt Sniffing (Tail gaiting).** Remind your teen to maintain Jungle spacing behind the vehicle ahead to buy themselves more time.
  - **Insufficient scanning.** Stress the importance of always knowing the location of other vehicles on the road. Scan ahead before making left turns, look and see left, right, left, right, and make sure to check the rear view mirror. And when making lane changes, (SMMS) signal, mirror, mirror, shoulder.

# Left Turn on Green

- **No. 8—Impaired driving.** Of all drivers between fifteen and twenty years of age involved in fatal crashes in 2007, nearly one out of three had been drinking. In the United States, it is illegal for anyone under age twenty-one to drink alcohol. All states have zero tolerance laws that ban underage drinking and driving. Most states will suspend or cancel the license of a teen that violates these laws. Strictly enforce zero tolerance laws at home, whether or not your teen driver is caught by law enforcement. Make sure, as a parent, that *you* set the proper example and *never* drink and drive!

# Chapter 10

## Big Brown

I resist using the word "expert" in writing this book, but I will tell you that I spent the majority of time in my adult life with a corporation dedicated to driver safety and performance – UPS, otherwise known as United Parcel Service.

UPS is one of the greatest and most successful American corporations in the world. The key to their over 100 years of success is the ability to be innovative, creative, and most importantly, embrace change by being flexible with their thinking and goal and strategy development. They have a fleet of 150,000 vehicles, an airline, and 400,000 plus employees that specialize in distribution of cargo, freight, goods, and logistics. I spent over twenty-four years playing an active role in helping UPS achieve their goals. Much of that time was spent training and helping employees to work and drive safely in the role of Health and Safety Manager. What I learned and experienced about driving and road safety over my career was very compelling and inspiring.

I tell you this story because I want you to know why I approach the task of keeping people alive in the highway Jungle differently than others do. As you might realize from previous exposure to drivers training programs and from earlier in this book, the roots of formalized drivers training in this country begin in the various state school systems. It was called drivers education and was taught by various faculty members of whatever school that was offering the service. Initially, it was free or for very little cost to the students. In some states the program was even subsidized by state governments in order to keep the tuition affordable.

Many of the readers of this book were products of these public school programs, including myself. As a matter of fact, when I took drivers education I was taught by my shop teacher. I can't remember much of what he taught me, or his name, but I do remember he was a pretty good guy. I also remember that it was free and I even believe I received a grade for the class. I think it was an A!

Over time, many private drivers education companies began to emerge as an option to the public school system. Many of these companies were started by former or retired educators who taught drivers ed. prior to retirement.

I attended Michigan State University and received a degree in Criminal Justice. Although I had an interest in working in a crime lab, my first choice was to become a high school teacher. I wanted to teach history and coach football and basketball. Unfortunately, my advisor informed me that the teaching market was flooded with teachers, and I would have a difficult time finding a position. As a result I changed my focus to police work. Ironically, when I graduated from college it just so

happened that there was a shortage of teachers. Isn't it funny how things work out?

Attending and graduating from MSU was one of the many defining moments in my life, as was having the privilege of working for UPS while I was earning my degree.

I will never forget my first day at UPS. It was toward the end of May, and it was very hot for the time of year. I had attended classes for the first half of the day and then played basketball for a couple of hours in the afternoon. I then rode my bicycle the usual thirteen miles home and planned to just take it easy for a little while. I had just sat down when my older brother came into the house. He told me he just had an interview at UPS and was hoping they would hire him. My brother had just returned home from the military after serving a tour in Vietnam and had been out looking for a job.

My response was, "What is UPS?" After explaining to me what sort of business it was, he said if I hurried over to the UPS building I might get an interview and possibly get a job with them. I was exhausted and had zero motivation to interview for anything, let alone a job.

I don't really remember what motivated me, but somehow I hopped on my bike and rode it the short six

135

miles to UPS. Talk about being in the right place at the right time, or maybe the wrong time! I was hired on the spot and they wanted me to start work that afternoon. As the job was being described to me I kept thinking, "Why am I here? I don't even want a job. My brother should be doing this." (By the way, UPS never hired him.)

Before I realized the scope of what I was doing, I was standing in a forty-foot semi-trailer full of packages, exhaust pipes, tires, buckets, and who knows what else. The trailer was divided half-way down from the ceiling by a set of ball bearing rollers that extended almost the entire length of the trailer. I was standing on a floor that was divided in sections; these sections were called doors and they rested on the lip of the rollers. My job was to unload everything in the top half, and as I worked my way to the front of the trailer I was supposed to lift the doors and then unload the bottom half of the trailer. The entire time I had to push the packages and other items along the rollers and out on to a conveyor belt so the other UPS workers could sort the items based on zip code as the conveyor belts took them away.

The temperature had to be over 100 degrees. The air was filled with cardboard dust from all the packages. Guess what? This was the first of four trailers I was supposed to unload during a three to four hour time span, not to mention several of the brown trucks that were also full of the same packages and miscellaneous items.

Fortunately, I wasn't going to have to unload the entire trailer by myself because there was another UPS worker in the trailer with me. His name was Tom. I was told to watch Tom for a little while, so I could learn the techniques he was using to unload the trailer. I was told that I was supposed to keep up with him, so we could finish the trailer at the same time. That was easier said than done because Tom was a total animal. Two new people unloading at the same time couldn't keep up with him.

I'm a very competitive person, and there was no way I was going to let Tom beat me to the end of the trailer. I said to myself, "I will be the first one out of this trailer if it kills me." I learned a very important lesson that day. Pain is not a fun thing! I was twenty-two years old and in very good physical shape. I considered myself an athlete. But after being in school all day, playing basketball, and riding my bike all over the place, I didn't have enough gas left in my tank.

After lifting and bending over and over again, my lower back hurt so bad I thought I was going to pass out. I was sweating so profusely that I was soaked from head to toe. Even my socks were wet. This was only after about twenty minutes on the job. The supervisor could see that I was out of gas and told me I could take a minute and go get a drink. I crawled out of the trailer a mere shadow of my former self and asked where the water was. The supervisor said there was a hose in the car wash tunnel and I could get a drink from it.

As I drank the hot rubbery tasting water (the hose had been lying on the pavement in the hot sun), I decided I was going to quit. I had never quit anything in my life, but I was tired, my back was killing me, and I didn't even want or need a job. I asked myself why I was even there in the first place! This was all my stupid brother's fault.

Soon, I heard a voice yelling at me to get back in the trailer. It was my supervisor and he seemed angry. Before I knew it, I was back unloading the trailer with Tom. I finished the shift and dragged myself out to the parking lot and rode my bike the six miles home. Let me tell you, it was the longest six miles I've ever pedaled.

I'll never forget that first day at UPS. Little did I know then that I would spend a good portion of my adult life enjoying the privilege of working with and growing personally and professionally with the greatest people and company that exists today. UPS is a grassroots organization that believes in promoting within. You could begin your career as a clerk and, if properly motivated, you could become the president of the company.

UPS became a way of life for my family and me. As time passed, I had various opportunities to grow and impact the organization while in various management positions. One of my responsibilities came to be that of the Health and Safety Manager. As the Safety Manager, I was responsible for a number of the safety-related areas that would have a direct impact on the safety attitudes of each and every person at UPS. These responsibilities included Defensive Driving, Skid Control, Safe Work Methods, Off Road Recovery, and Accident Investigation and Reconstruction. Although very rewarding personally and professionally, the road to success in the safety field is closely associated with tragedy and sadness. Some of the accidents I investigated were some of the most mind-numbing experiences an individual could ever witness. As a professional, I would always attempt to maintain my composure, but to this day the memories from some of the tragic scenes I witnessed are firmly imbedded in my memory and will never be forgotten.

UPS is the largest transportation company in the world and its drivers travel millions of road miles every year. UPS drivers are the most thoroughly trained and efficient drivers in the world. All of them take extreme pride in their safety accomplishments. As a result, UPS drivers have accident frequencies ten times less than any of their competitors. What I learned about safe driving from UPS during my many years there was that safe and responsible driving is important at all levels: personal vehicles, business vehicles…any vehicle that is on the road. The skills I learned, and what I experienced while being part of UPS, were very helpful in developing *The Jungle Way* of driving.

There are many people who have spent many years instructing teens on how to drive a car the right way. As a matter of fact, I was at my favorite barbershop the other day getting a trim, and I was having a discussion with my barber about Jungle and about all the great comments he gets from his customers regarding Jungle Survival.

As I was answering my barber's questions, I was glancing around the room and I noticed a middle-aged gentleman sitting across the small room intently listening to our discussion. After a few moments, he spoke up and informed us that he had been a drivers education instructor for over thirty years and had worked for the public schools and with various private drivers education companies. As he spoke very proudly about the impressive numbers of teens he had trained over his career, I actively listened to his philosophy regarding teenagers and the approach that he and his fellow instructors used to teach them to drive. It didn't take me long to realize he was sharing his vast knowledge with me in effort to teach me about the correct way (in his mind) and the most effective way to teach teenagers how to drive. He was doing this without the slightest idea about my background and experience through UPS and Jungle. It was as if the way he taught teens was the only way and the best way. Since he was educating me as to the correct and most effective way to teach teenagers how to drive, I thought I would ask him a question or two.

I'm always interested in the how and why aspect of doing things a certain way. I have always believed in continuous improvement in everything I do. I have a simple philosophy: if you don't get better, you get worse. I asked the sage across the room why he did things the way he did and his answer was typical. "It was always the way it was done before I got there, and I just continued with the same process." I just took a deep breath, counted to ten under my breath and changed the discussion to an unrelated topic. To my relief, he withdrew from further discussion and continued reading his newspaper.

Don't get me wrong. I've always believed that learning how to get better is an art. I listened to the gentleman at the barbershop partly to be polite, and hopefully to learn something new that would help me to be more effective in my quest to keep these young people alive. But, part of getting better is to learn what not to do as well as what is right to do. Imagine if everyone's philosophy was, "That's the way it was always done and that's the way I do it." I've never accepted the status quo as a reason for doing anything. If I could find a better, more effective way of teaching teens and parents how to stay alive in the highway Jungle, I would instantly scrap what I've been teaching for over thirty years and adopt the better way.

This way, *The Jungle Way*, works and it has proven highly effective. It has become my message, my life, and what I believe in.

# Chapter 11

## The Right Way... *The Jungle Way*

I am often asked, "What makes Jungle different from other driving schools?" Jungle doesn't just teach you how to drive a car; we teach you how to survive in a car.

This is the heart of *The Jungle Way* of driving the teenagers can relate to. We have developed a way to drive that is different and unique – we make no excuses or explanations of that. We believe it engages the teen to learn, to establish a safe driving skill set, and have an overriding safety-conscious attitude on the road, which will help him or her to survive. That is our bottom line!

To make it simple, let's define our three ways to drive a car the right way. Phase one is about the lines, signs, markings, and the laws. Phase Two is how to operate a car. This would include starting, maneuvering a car through traffic, turning, stopping, and understanding how a car works. Phase Three is what most people think that driving a car is all about and is only developed over time with experience. Phase Three is the most important phase and the most challenging and beneficial to learn. It involves learning how to survive in the highway Jungle and driving to protect everyone else in the car and on the road. Learning this phase requires desire, motivation, and the right attitude. Unfortunately, many of the wild animals driving in the Jungle already think they are driving the right way. Therefore, they don't see a reason to change to a different way of driving.

Most people, including parents, have a preconceived notion as to what learning to drive a car is all about. Their perception, as described earlier, is based on their own experiences when they first learned to drive as teenagers. This is where the previously explained "Good Driver Syndrome" stands as a huge roadblock to *The Jungle Way* of driving.

*The Jungle Way* has been proven to be an extremely effective approach to greatly reducing the number of auto accidents and the associated deaths and injuries. Due to the fact that *The Jungle Way* is the opposite of how most animals drive in the Jungle, it is not an easy task converting an experienced driver to a Jungle driver. Adapting and adjusting to a different way of doing anything relates to the human condition of being resistant to change. The only motivation for change is directly related to the benefit an individual will receive if they change. If the effort it takes to change is greater than the outcome, change will not take place.

Ask a parent who has suffered the loss of child due to an auto accident this simple question: "Prior to your teenager being killed or crippled in an auto accident, if you had known there was a better way for them to learn to drive that would have kept them out of harm's way, would you have enrolled them in such a program?" We all know what the answer would be!

The goal of most parents is to raise their children to be happy, successful, healthy, and safe. What more could you as a parent hope for? But, for these things to happen there needs to be more than hope; there needs to be commitment, involvement, quality training, accountability, mentoring, consistency, and fun. The reason I mention the goal of most parents is because I believe there are parents who should have never had children in the first place. They are poorly equipped to provide these vital nurturing elements so important to the future of their children, and in many cases the results are often tragic.

I know you are probably wondering why I'm on a soapbox lecturing you about the proper way to raise children. Hey, my wife and I made our share of mistakes raising our three children, but we think they turned out pretty good in spite of those mistakes. I write about these things because learning and driving a motor vehicle should be a positive and enjoyable family experience. It shouldn't and doesn't need to turn into a nightmare of an experience because things weren't done right in the beginning. At this point, I think it would be meaningful if I spent some time discussing these nurturing aspects I previously mentioned as the keys to your children's positive future.

## Commitment

I've always felt that commitment is one of the more complex and difficult words to define as it can mean different things to different people. Rather than becoming sidetracked, I'll explain commitment as it relates to teenagers who become part of *The Jungle Way* driving experience.

Let's first talk about the commitment of the parents. Most parents are totally committed to their children. Their primary focus in their life is insuring the well-being of their children. This commitment should be evident when they decide it's time for their son or daughter to drive a motor vehicle. The decision to allow their teen to drive should never be taken lightly. After all, they are teenagers and we already know they lack several qualities and capabilities needed for them to be effective drivers of a three- to four-thousand pound missile!

We already know teens lack the frontal lobe development of the brain. This prevents them from being able to properly plan and organize their activities. They lack the ability to prioritize effectively, or simply stated, determine what is important or not at any given time. They have an added burden of applying inappropriate logic and rationale when attempting to make sound decisions. This causes them to make spontaneous decisions without the use of an effective thought process, and many times they make decisions with no thought at all.

Who should know their teenagers better than their own committed and involved parents? These parents should be committed to making sure they are making the correct decisions in allowing their teen to begin the process of driving a vehicle. This commitment should involve researching and selecting the most effective training program available. This is not done by having their teen pick up a phone book and call all of the drivers training schools in the phone book in an attempt to find the cheapest one.

Committed parents don't allow their teens to enroll in a drivers education program because their best friend wants them to go there. The parent needs to base their decision of where their teen will take their training based on their own first-hand investigation process. During their research and investigation they should ask the right questions of the school they are interviewing, including the following:

1. What are your statistics regarding your graduated students and their parents?

Their response will most likely be, "What statistics are you talking about?" You will have totally confused them at this point. They will tell you how many students they have trained and how long they've been in business, how many locations they have, the type of vehicles they use, or how many awards their instructors have received.

A good driving school should be able to provide you with a number of important statistics which help the school determine their quality and effectiveness of training. Statistics such as the percentage and type of accidents their students are experiencing after receiving their license, number and type of tickets, cell phone usage of students and parents, friends in the car, and many more. If they are unable to provide this type of information, then this is a telling sign they are only interested in the number of students that enroll in their school so they can make a profit.

2. What type of training do you provide for parents?

3. Do you provide follow up training after students have graduated if they are struggling, or have experienced any accidents? If so, what does the training include, and is there a cost?

4. If a student should be involved in an auto accident after receiving their license, do you provide any accident investigation service? If so, is there a cost?

I hope you understand the point I'm trying to make, which is the fact that you could go through the entire phone book and call every driving school in the book and none of them would be able to provide you with any of this information. They would wonder if you were some sort of news group or an investigating agency trying to check up on them.

If you called Jungle Survival Drivers Training, all of these questions would be answered with statistics based on annual surveys that Jungle conducts with their families to determine if we are as effective as we think we are in keeping our students out of harm's way. Jungle Survival's commitment to your children is second to none. We are constantly striving to get better at what we do. One of our philosophies is if you don't get better, you get worse. I have always said that if I could find or develop a system that would be more effective at saving these young lives, then I would scrap *The Jungle Way* and adopt the new system!

Jungle's commitment to our students and parents is never-ending. We never fail a student because we continue driving with our students after they complete Jungle if they are struggling with the process of learning to drive a motor vehicle *The Jungle Way*.

Our students are proud to have graduated from Jungle Survival. They believe that *The Jungle Way* is the cool way to drive. They are committed to driving *The Jungle Way* to save their lives, their friend's and families' lives, and the lives of other motorists in the highway Jungle.

## Involvement

Jungle understands that no matter how well we train our students to drive *The Jungle Way*, without the complete and long-term involvement of the parents, all of our efforts will be in vain. Parents hold the key to the ultimate driving success of their teenager. Parents are like the Holy Grail when it comes to their teen's chances of survival in the highway Jungle.

Sometimes it becomes necessary to use various motivational techniques to achieve the required level of involvement needed to reach success, and many times your reputation precedes you as in the follow story.

# "I Want the Best"

I had a mother call me the other day; she wanted to ask me some questions about the requirements in Michigan that her son would have to meet in order to get a drivers license. She and her family were moving from Wisconsin to Michigan, and she wanted to know how long it would take her son to get his license.

She had a beautiful English accent, and since I had lived in England for a few years, I asked her how long she had been in the United States. She indicated she had been in the States for about five years. She explained that she was very apprehensive about her son learning to drive since he had just turned fifteen. Even though he was a very bright and mature young man, he was still very young. She said drivers training in Europe is taken very seriously, and in most countries you have to be eighteen before you can enroll in a drivers training program. The programs are more expensive, but they are worth the extra money.

I asked her what level of parent involvement the training programs in England required. This question must have confused her because she wanted to know why any drivers training school would involve the parents other than to pay for the classes. She explained to me that in Wisconsin, where they currently lived, there was no requirement for parent involvement, other than the parents must drive with their teen for a period of time after they complete drivers training. I said that that was similar to what is required in Michigan. I could tell she was becoming more confused by the second to the point of frustration, so I decided to explain to her philosophy of driving *The Jungle Way*.

As I went through my explanation step-by-step, she didn't say a word. At one point, I had to pause and ask her if she was still there. I would periodically ask her if she understood and if she had any questions. Still thinking she was confused, I decided to ask her my usual question of how she had heard of Jungle Survival. She told me that when she went to the administration office at the school her son would be attending after they moved from Wisconsin, she asked the secretary at the front desk whom the school would recommend for drivers training. The secretary asked her to wait a moment while she checked with the other people in the office. She said after a few seconds a group of people came out into the front of the office from the back offices and excitedly yelled, "Jungle is the place! Jungle is the best there is! They teach the kids how to survive and stay alive! Don't go anywhere else!"

She said that experience is what inspired her to contact Jungle. She said I didn't need to explain everything to her and she just wanted to find out how long it would take for her son to be able to drive by himself. She had made up her mind where he was going to take drivers training before she even called. She researched all of the other drivers training schools in the area and found there was no comparison between any of them and Jungle. She wanted to feel confident that she sent her son to a place that cared about keeping him alive and not just getting paid. That is why she selected Jungle.

Stories like these have become commonplace over the years, but you can never get too full of yourself when you're dealing with the young and fragile lives of our future. It can all come crashing down around you if tragedy strikes. In many cases, when it does, emotions take over. Feelings of despair, sorrow, helplessness, and frustration fill the air. I tell you this because it happened to me. One of my former students made a fatal mistake which caused the death of another young driver and injury to himself. I will tell that story in Chapter 15.

## Quality Training *The Jungle Way*

An overview of *The Jungle Way* of driving will significantly improve your teen's chances of survival in the highway Jungle! Survival, as the title of this book suggests, is the goal. We all know road accidents are inevitable, but it has to be the goal to reduce or eliminate the crippling statistics of teen driving accidents, or our mission is useless. I'm stating this fact based on the results Jungle has achieved over the last seven years. As I confirmed earlier, the leading cause of death to teenagers in this country is auto accidents. In the first one to three years of driving, 80% of all teens will be involved in some type of auto accident. In the first twelve months of driving, one out of six sixteen-year-olds will have a serious accident. Only 10% of Jungle students experience an auto accident during their first one to three years of driving, and in seven years of teaching teens *The Jungle Way* of driving, not one

Jungle student has died or been seriously injured as a result of an auto accident.

We learn from the statistics that there is great room for improvement, and *The Jungle Way* of driving with its deeper philosophy of safety and survival is essential to reducing the number of teens who are killed and crippled or who, as a result of their unsafe action, kill or cripple others. The teenagers of our generation and their children will be the lifelong benefactors of this approach to learning to drive.

One of Jungle's first slogans was "Saving Lives One Family at a Time!" and based on our results, we have saved countless young lives. This statement raises the question. How do you know if you saved a life if no one dies? The answer can be found in the following story. I'll just call it "The First Dollar Earned."

## "The First Dollar Earned"

When people start their own business, their obvious goals are to make a profit and provide the best products, or services available. One old tradition that has survived over the years is when a business earns its first dollar, that dollar is framed and placed in a conspicuous place to commemorate that accomplishment.

At Jungle we also need to make a profit in order to continue our efforts of saving young lives. Earning our first dollar wasn't our primary goal, but saving a life was. That elusive goal was achieved on a beautiful Sunday afternoon while one of my young students who had recently graduated from Jungle was waiting at a busy intersection at a red light.

Lenora loved to drive, and on this particular day she convinced her father to go with her for a leisurely drive around her small community. Lenora was a very over-confident young driver due to the fact that she had driven extensively with her father before coming to Jungle. That's right; she drove illegally and for quite some time. When she enrolled in Jungle, her father explained to me that Lenora had been driving for a couple of years and had probably driven over 3,000 miles. This previous experience and the habits she had formed made it very difficult to Jungalize Lenora. You have to remember that it's impossible to teach a person habits. It's only possible to teach the correct methods, and this is accomplished by the conscious and repetitive use of these methods until they become habits.

I definitely had to use the "sell not tell" approach to Jungalizing Lenora. By the time she graduated from Jungle, she understood and applied *The Jungle Way* of driving which made her fully Jungalized!

Back to the story. Lenora was heading westbound on a divided highway with her father riding shotgun. The posted speed limit was 55 mph, but the average speed for vehicles on this stretch of highway was between 60 and 70 mph. As a matter of fact, this one-mile stretch Lenora was driving on was a well-known speed trap area with county  monitoring the flow of traffic.

Lenora decided to make a left turn at the next traffic light, now heading southbound. The light was red, and Lenora made a complete stop. (Remember the bounce back.) Another vehicle pulled up alongside of her on her right, but stopped past the stop line. At this particular traffic light, vehicles can only go straight or southbound. The highway is one-way heading east with no left turn permitted. The vehicles heading north can only turn right, also eastbound. The speed limit in all directions is 55 mph. All of these factors make this intersection one of the more dangerous in the area. Over the years there have been countless accidents at the very spot Lenora was waiting. Across the intersection from where Lenora was stopped was a stump of an old telephone pole. It stood there as a result of a previous fatal accident. A green piece of electrical wire from the car that struck it runs all the way through the

The light turned green, and even though the highway was one way, Lenora looked left, right, left, and then right again as she was taught in Jungle. When she completed the second left, she noticed a speeding car heading the wrong way toward her. The car to her right took off as soon as the light had turned green, and the speeding car struck her broadside and flipped her car over several times. Lenora had never moved from the intersection because she saw the car coming.

I was in my living room at home when a hysterical and tearful Lenora called me and tried to explain how *The Jungle Way* had saved her and her father's lives. It was difficult to understand her, so I asked to speak to her father. He was a little calmer and he shared with me the circumstances surrounding the accident. His actual statement to me was, "At first I didn't realize what had just happened because it happened too fast. A blur flew in front of us from the left; I heard a very loud thud and saw a car flipping over next to us. After a few seconds, I realized what had happened. Lenora's actions had most likely saved our lives. Jungle saved our lives."

Somehow, the local newspaper found out about the details surrounding the accident and called to ask me for an interview. The reporter was so intrigued by the entire story that she decided to write a feature story that appeared on the front page of the Sunday edition. That story hangs on our wall at Jungle, in a frame, signed by Lenora. Jungle's first dollar had been earned!

# Situational Driving

My primary objective when I started the Jungle was to save as many lives as possible by motivating young people to drive for everyone in the car and everybody on the road. I wanted everyone to drive with more patience, courtesy, and professionalism than everyone else in the Jungle. In more basic terms, drive the opposite of everyone else on the road. This starts and ends with "situational driving."

As I related to you earlier in the book, as a Health and Safety Manager for UPS for much of my twenty-four-year career, I had several responsibilities. My primary responsibility was to teach defensive driving skills to the drivers and management. In addition, I taught skid control techniques, off-road recovery, and was responsible for auto accident investigations and reconstruction. Auto accident investigations were one of the most interesting tasks I had to perform, but also the most depressing.

Whenever I would be required to investigate an accident, I would assemble a team of people to assist in the investigation, and at the same time I would teach them the proper auto accident investigation techniques. Many of the accidents were of a very serious nature involving loss of life and severe injuries. Our responsibility was to determine who was at fault in order to minimize exposure to various liability concerns. If the accident involved a fatality, it always had a very sobering effect on the investigation team. The younger the victims, the more of an impact it would have on all of us. We all felt completely helpless, and all we could do was ask why. Why so young?

In order to reduce the number of these accidents, our drivers would be involved in a defensive driving process I taught. It reduced accidents by almost 70%, a significant reduction to say the least. Imagine the number of lives saved as a result.

Most people have heard of the words "defensive driving," and if you look in any local phone book you will discover that most driving schools claim to teach defensive driving skills. If you called them, they would tell you their defensive driving class is approved by some various national organizations with "safety" in their title. They will tell you that their class is a certain number of hours, and upon completion of the class you will receive a certificate of completion. Usually, the training is conducted entirely in a classroom and last for around four hours. This is a totally ineffective approach to effectively teaching anyone how to drive defensively!

Most people who are interested in paying for a defensive driving class have no interest in becoming better drivers, but are taking the class as a result of a court order, due to a certain number of points on their driving record, or maybe a as requirement of their employer. The letter of completion is their primary reason for taking the class.

"Defensive driving" is a conceptual process where the driver is taught to manage time and space around their vehicle. The Smith System and the SIPDE System (Search, Identify, Predict, Decide, and Execute) are the two primary processes used to teach defensive driving. I have taught both systems and although they are both effective, I decided early on that The Smith System was much more specific in its methodology than the SIPDE System. This specificity makes it much easier to practice and apply the methods allowing students to develop the correct habits and correct style of driving.

I always felt that something was missing from both approaches that diminished their level of effectiveness. I have taught the Smith System for over thirty years and recently came to the conclusion that, although it is a very effective approach to teaching defensive driving, there is room for improvement. The premise of the Smith System is based on the fact that an individual operating a motor vehicle should be focused and attentive while driving. Simply stated, they must think about driving while driving! Unfortunately, the opposite is usually true.

Most drivers are thinking about everything else but driving. Their only thought and resulting reaction is when they are suddenly faced with a driving problem that requires a split second decision to avoid an accident. Their response is to slam on the brakes or swerve, and maybe the driver of the other vehicle does the same. If a collision is avoided, then it was just a close call. Sometimes a driver will attribute their ability to avoid such a situation to the lightening quick reactions and skill he or she possesses. It was more likely due to something called "being lucky." The results of such a response are much too reactionary and unrealistic to expect a consistent application by most drivers.

The belief that an individual operating a motor vehicle can remain focused and attentive while driving is inaccurate. Just ask yourself one question. How consistently focused on driving a three- to four-thousand pound missile am I when I drive? I think we all know the answer!

I should have come to this conclusion much sooner, but I ironically developed tunnel vision in my thinking and my philosophy that once you think you're good, you never get better. This should never happen!

I made the statement earlier in the book that I've learned more from my young students than I've learned from any school, or training seminar. My students have reshaped and molded what Jungle is today by changing the way I look at things, and I'm sure they will continue to do so in the future. As a result of the realization that the defensive driving approach I had used for so many years would not be effective with teenage drivers, I decided it was time to approach the challenge of teaching teens to drive from a different angle. I realized that no matter what I taught my students, they were still going to do what teens do in a car. I needed to instill in them a style of driving that would fit their level of maturity and thought process.

The combination of their physiological inability to stay focused, their overconfidence, and their inexperience behind the wheel are what cause so many of them to be killed or crippled, or to kill and cripple others. What do teens do in a car? Much the same as what experienced adult drivers do in a car! Eat, drink, talk to passengers, listen to music, talk and text on cell phones, fall asleep, daydream, smoke, and more. Combine these distractions and many more with an inexperienced, overconfident, teenager lacking a frontal lobe development in the brain and you have a formula for disaster!

*The Jungle Way* of driving takes all of these factors into account. By teaching the correct proactive driving methods to the teenager when they first learn to drive, they will develop a driving style that fits them. For example, when approaching an intersection teens reach their "Point of Decision" prior to entering the intersection. At this point they remove their foot from the accelerator, shadow the brake, look left, right, left, right, check their mirrors and, when clear, they proceed through the intersection. They do this automatically because it was ingrained during their first thirty days of driving, and it became one of their driving habits and part of their normal driving style.

Instead of "defensive driving" we teach "situational driving." What does this mean? In "defensive driving", drivers are taught to see and react. In "situational driving", we develop awareness before it happens to proactively deal with anything that a driver could encounter. And what exactly is this? It is a combination of many things in *The Jungle Way*, and it emphasizes situational awareness on the road and in the car. It may sound simple, but it truly is a skill set which has to be developed and learned by any driver.

This is why the education and involvement of the parents is so crucial to the successful application of *The*

*Jungle Way* of driving. The parents have to provide the focused accountability during the first thirty days of driving with their teen. Ideally, it would be great if the parents changed the way they drive to *The Jungle Way*, but I realized early on that this change wasn't going to happen very often due to the simple fact that you can't teach old dogs new tricks!

# Chapter 12

## Does Anybody Here Speak Teenager?

My first class had seven students and I realized very quickly that I had to drastically alter my approach if I was going to be successful teaching them *The Jungle Way* of driving. Why, you may ask? Because we are dealing with teenagers! I had to adjust, and think counter-intuitively regarding the "animal" I was going to tame. (Just kidding – no I'm totally serious!) If teenagers were the focus, I needed to learn and educate myself about what kind of "customer" I was dealing with.

I quickly learned it was all about communication – I had to learn to speak the language of teenagers, with emphasis in the adolescent dialect and accent. I had a big task ahead of me, but this was key to relaying my message to teens, and is at the heart of the program.

My mind needed to become "teenagerized", another original Jungle word. Being "teenagerized" is the complex process where the adult mind is reconditioned to think like a teenager. You might be thinking that this seems kind of silly, but this process is very similar to what a salesperson might use when they are attempting to sell his products or services to a potential customer.

A successful salesperson knows that it takes several factors in order to make a sale whether he is selling product or a service. The product or service must be of the highest quality and better than what they are currently using, cost effective, and simple to integrate into their company. The customer needs to be educated as to how the product or service will help or improve their business and be needed by them. They also need to be encouraged to try the new product or service after they have already used a competitor's products or services. Most important to success at selling is being able to look at the potential sale from the perspective of the customer. In other words, think as if you were the customer and listen to what your customer is saying.

I learned early on in my professional career while working at UPS that listening to and understanding how people think and perceive various situations is crucial to being an effective motivator and trainer. This was especially important if Jungle was going to be remotely effective. Teens presented a unique and challenging opportunity for me when I opened Jungle and they still do to this day.

Having spent the majority of my adult life working for UPS, my brain has been wired to operate in a certain way, somewhat rigid and similar to "It's my way or the highway" mentality. One of my favorite communication tools I utilized in my position as a UPS Safety Manager was PowerPoint presentations. Naturally, it was the first thing I thought of using while I was planning my class lesson plans. I thought my students would love it. I would include all of the cool graphics and jungle sounds, and it would be very visual. I always knew that people learn more effectively through visualization.

Prior to beginning my first Jungle class, I thought it would be a great idea if my dear wife Jane and I took a vacation to Cancun. We booked a one-week escape to our favorite resort, The Paradisus Riviera Cancun. It's a very romantic, tranquil, and relaxing place. It is a place where we could get away and spend some quality time together. I thought maybe I could even do a little work on my PowerPoint presentation when Jane wasn't looking.

I honestly never intended to spend too much time on the presentation; I was just going to get it started. After all, I only use my two middle fingers when I type, and I would use the time efficiently and productively. So, I packed my trusty laptop as my wife rolled her eyes and muttered something like, "I knew it!"

Unfortunately I got a little carried away and spent the majority of the get away vacation at our beautiful resort converting the entire textbook I was intending to use with my class into a PowerPoint presentation. Fortunately, Jane knows how to enjoy herself despite the fact that I'm an idiot, and she said she had a great time anyway with all the new friends she met! Isn't that odd? I never met one of them!

The first day of my first class was the only time I ever used the presentation. I was so excited to show it off to my new students that I forgot all about them sitting in the room being forced to endure such agony. I was so excited about my masterpiece that I didn't even consider if my students, my customers, were interested in what I was doing. I had my trusty laser pointer, my cool sounds and graphics, but I didn't have them! It was a disaster to say the least.

Fortunately for me and the future of Jungle, I had a young man in the class who also happened to be my first student to enroll in Jungle. He was the son of my neighbor, friend, and my first employee. The student's name was Paul and I had known him since he was a little boy. He was and still is an awesome young man. I thought I would ask him after class what he and the other students thought of the PowerPoint presentation. I was sure he would say that it was the coolest thing they had ever seen. When I asked him what he and the others thought of the presentation, he looked at me with a very nervous grin and said the following: "It was bad, very bad. It was so bad that if you showed it again they would all walk out of the class. As a matter of fact, it was so boring we came very close to walking out of the room while your back was turned on us."

At that moment, after I overcame my shock, I realized that for Jungle to work I had to mentally become a teenager. I had to teach myself how to think, perceive, react, and relate to what teens were all about. That first class of seven taught me more about young people than I could have ever dreamed. They "teenagerized" me and ultimately are the reasons why Jungle has become so successful at saving teen lives. Parents must learn from this model – understand your teenager, and a safer driver is the result when approached properly.

Understanding the teenager was the key to my business being a success and reaching our goal – helping to save lives.

## "Jungalizing the Unfocused Teenager"

The dictionary defines focus as "a concentrated effort or attention on a particular thing." In short, how long can an individual pay attention? A high school teacher with thirty years of experience once told me that you can only expect one minute of focus for each year of age when working with teenagers. So, with a fifteen-year-old you can only expect them to pay attention for fifteen minutes, and not all at one time.

This inability to pay attention for a sustained period of time is based on several factors. By the way, lack of focus is not an issue reserved for just teenagers. Many of us can lose focus from time to time; it's what makes us human. Lack of focus can be caused by boredom, lack of interest, internal and external distractions, developmental brain issues, alcohol, drugs, etc.

Operating a motor vehicle, one of the most dangerous things a human being can do, requires a great deal of focus. Think of it this way. The average driver makes approximately thirty driving decisions per minute and for every 500 decisions, they make one mistake. That mistake doesn't necessarily result in a collision or a close call, and in most cases will go largely unnoticed by the individual, or passengers in the car.

An Individual ultimately becomes involved in a collision or close call as a result of too many mistakes taking place over a period of time. Just remember, the only difference between a close call and a collision is that not enough things go wrong at the right time to cause a collision. You might hit your brakes or swerve, or if another driver is involved, they might hit their brakes and swerve at just the right time making it just a close call.

Most drivers operate their vehicle with less focus than it takes to brush their teeth in the morning. Driving a vehicle becomes such a routine that there is virtually no thought relating to the challenges and skills it takes to operating a three- to four-thousand pound missile that can kill and injure themselves and others.

Added to this lack of focus is the fact that most people were never really taught properly how to operate a motor vehicle in the first place. Just ask anyone what they remember when they first learned to drive. They might say things like "hands at ten and two on the steering wheel" or "one car length following distance for every ten miles per hour." As experienced and self-professed good drivers, they don't do either of the things they remember being taught.

A teenager's lack of focus is in large part due to their age. Studies have shown that teenagers between the ages of thirteen and nineteen tend to act irrationally and impulsively. They don't make the best decisions and do things more spontaneously than an adult. There has been a great deal of research done which provides evidence as to why teenagers struggle with correct decision-making abilities.

The frontal lobes, located at the front of the cranium, are the area of the brain that control rational behavior and reasoning. This area for teenagers is not fully developed until they reach their mid-twenties. So, their decision-making capabilities and lack of focus are caused by a physiological development problem in the brain. This lack of brain development is present in males and females. In females, this area of the brain develops sooner than with males. Most people have always believed that girls mature faster than boys, and they are correct.

Lack of decision-making and focusing ability are obviously serious problems when we decide to drive a car. An experienced adult driver has a better chance of surviving due to their ability to prioritize and focus at a more consistent level than teenagers. This brain development issue is one of the primary reasons it is so difficult to produce teenage drivers who drive with the right attitude, but it's not impossible to produce teenager drivers who drive in a focused, courteous, and skilled manner. It can and is being done with the active, hands-on, and properly directed involvement of parents.

It has been suggested that the minimum age to drive a car should be raised to eighteen. This has been done in many parts of Europe. In the United States, some states have raised the age to seventeen. Obviously, raising the age would pretty much fix the teenage driving problem, but is it necessary? I firmly believe teenagers can be taught to drive the correct way if the parents are given the right training and long-term support. I believe this because that is what *The Jungle Way* of driving is all about.

Maintaining focus for any of us is not an easy task. Internal and external influences cause us to drift in many different directions. The challenge of working with teenagers is a constant struggle to hold their interest for sustained periods of time. Many times I feel like an orchestra conductor might feel when his orchestra is out of sync and he can't get every musician to play the musical piece in harmony.

Teaching *The Jungle Way* to teens is similar and equally as challenging while in the classroom. I find myself having to be as much of an entertainer as well as a teacher, coach, and friend. I many times have to trick my students into learning. Let me give you a little example.

# "Mom Or Dad, Are You Listening?"

I had just finished class one day, and as I was cleaning up and turning out the lights, I noticed one of my students was standing at the edge of the room watching me. I initially thought he was just waiting for his parents to pick him up after class. He waited until I was almost ready to leave and approached me with an unusual request. He wanted me to speak with his mother about my thoughts regarding the frontal lobe development in the brain of teenagers. He explained to me that his mother had an entirely different take on the subject of frontal lobe development and she was driving him crazy.

The question, I'm sure, came as a result of an earlier discussion we had during class regarding the challenges I faced in my efforts to Jungalize teenagers. "Jungalizing" is a term I use to describe the process used in Jungle to sell and motivate my students on *The Jungle Way* of driving. I explained to the class that "Jungalization" was a difficult task to accomplish due to their lack of frontal lobe development in the cortex of the brain.

He was a very perceptive, focused, and persistent young man who had created a very strong and positive impression with me. He always asked very thought-provoking questions. I asked him what his mother was doing that was so bad it was driving him crazy. He remembered the class discussion of my explanation of teenage frontal lobe development and the lack of total development preventing teenagers from having the ability to plan and organize. He was extremely irritated by his mother constantly pushing him to plan and organize his time better. She felt it would be a big advantage to him if he could teach himself to be more effective regarding his planning and organizational skills.

I explain to my students that I believe they are a product of their environment, and the way they ultimately turn out is a result of the way their parents raised them. I always tell them, jerky kids come from jerky parents and good kids come from good parents. I shared this thought with him, but as in many cases with teenagers, it went in one ear and out the other.

A few minutes passed and I was focusing my attention on getting the place cleaned up for the following day, and the next thing I knew, the young man was standing in front of me with both of his parents. As I said, he was very persistent and he was bound and determined to have me explain to his mother why she was wrong about her harassment of him with respect to his poor planning and organizational skills.

He began to tell her that teenagers were unable to plan and organize effectively because they lack frontal lobe development in the brain and that is where all of their planning capabilities come from. She indicated she knew about frontal lobe development, but didn't want to discuss it with him at the moment. He looked at me and said, "Tell her what you told us in class." Talk about putting someone on the spot. I was briefly at a loss for words because I didn't want to say anything that would make it sound like I was contradicting his mother.

Before I could say anything, he said he was tired of her lecturing him for forty-five minutes at a time about the same old thing. He said after the first few minutes of one of her lectures about what a poor planner he is, he just tunes her out. He explained to her that I was always getting off on tangents in class and spent time talking about unrelated topics instead of lecturing the class for an hour about the same thing. As a result, it was more interesting and easier to learn and remember things, plus it was a lot more fun.

He was unaware that he had just summarized in a sentence one aspect of my Jungalization process I utilize with my students. By keeping them engaged with a variety of topics, I'm able to sneak into the discussion the important topics I really want to have them learn. I like to say that it's best to keep them off balance so they always are wondering what's next.

He was working himself up pretty good, and I could see that his parents were also becoming agitated and embarrassed at the same time. I had to resolve this quickly so I looked at him and said, "Why do you think you turned out so well? You are an awesome young man with a lot going for you. I, for one, am very impressed with you and it's a real pleasure having you in my class. The reason you are who you are is due to these two people standing next to you. They packed a whole lot of good stuff into you over the seventeen years you've been on this earth and you owe them a great deal. As a matter of fact, do you ever give your mom or dad a hug and tell them you love them? There is nothing you can do that will make a parent happier than that."

He explained to me he tells them he loves them when he does something wrong and apologizes to them. I said, "Do you ever do it for no reason other than you just want to let them know how you feel?" His response was a quiet no. I told him not to disregard his mother's attempts to get him to be a better planner and organizer. She was right to push him because his brain can be wired to enable him to become an effective planner and organizer if he sticks with it.

Jungalizing teenagers is a complex task due to many factors and their lack of focusing ability is at the top of the list. In many cases, more than a third of the students in any one of my classes have a variety of learning challenges. In addition to the lack of frontal lobe development, they can have ADD, ADHD, dyslexia, various syndromes, autism, hearing loss, vision issues, physical challenges, bi-polar disorder, anxiety disorders, depression, or just having a crush on the girl or guy sitting across the room.

Many of these teenagers are on various medications, and by the time they get to their Jungle class their medication has worn off. On top of that, they have been in school for the last eight hours with only a few hours of sleep.

Yes, teenagers may go to bed, but they don't go to sleep right away. You see there is this thing called technology. Let's see, cell phones, iTouch or iPods, obviously computers and computer games, Xbox 360, Playstation 3, PSP, and of course, you have to update your Facebook status every twenty minutes and chat for a while

with your friends. For the more serious students, studying and doing homework is squeezed in.

At Jungle we stress focus, attention, and avoiding distractions. Knowing how these areas are manifested in the teenager's mind helps us to direct emphasis on how to apply the tools of Jungle to prevent negative consequences while a teen drives.

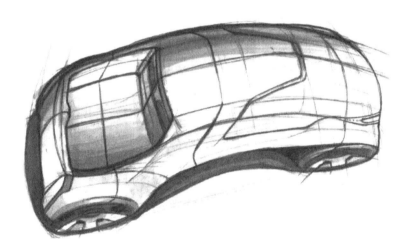

# Chapter 13

## The Student

One of my best students in all of the many thousands I have trained is Samir, a young Bosnian refuge who came to America after fleeing the civil war that had torn the Baltic's apart. He, interestingly enough, comes from a family of professional truck drivers in their homeland. They are very hard-working, good people who have taken their skills and dreams to America and now work as truck drivers in Michigan. They saw the importance of a proper and grounded drivers education program for Samir, and after careful research and consideration they chose Jungle.

Even after all of these years, I am amazed at what I can learn from my students. Unfortunately, many adults have the attitude that just because they are older they can't learn anything useful from someone so much younger than them. The lessons that this fine young man taught me were invaluable. He had the right attitude – one willing to absorb and learn. And he knew the value and importance of good, safe driving skills, obviously passed down from his parents and family members over the years. I thought for a moment and then understood that, no matter where ever you are driving in the world, no matter what road, paved or unpaved, highway or country road, safe driving is so very important. I realized through this young man that driving skills mattered regardless of what country you lived in around the world or what road you were on.

I thought a lot about the variety of teens that have attended Jungle over the years with all of the different backgrounds, races, nationalities, and upbringings. All had one thing in common: they were young teens with their lives ahead of them with unlimited possibilities. That is why I wrote in the beginning of this book – safe driving skills are a gift we as parents can give to our children so they can take it with them forever in their lives.

Someday these teens are going to be driving around in SUVs and Minivans as mothers and fathers taking their kids somewhere, or renting a car on vacation in Spain, or on a business trip in Seattle. Or, maybe they will just be driving to or from work, or to a ballgame. Every situation matters, and the rules and principles of safe driving to survive *The Jungle Way* still apply. *The Jungle Way* is a message which stretches across any border, any country, or any nationality…to any place in the world where driving automobiles and increasing safety is a goal.

# Chapter 14

## Are You Listening?

While developing the methods I use for Jungalizing my students, I immediately realized the most important method is to actively listen to them when they talk. You see, most people are not what I call active listeners. An active listener is someone who looks you square in the eye while you are speaking with them and will always ask questions to clarify, or encourage you to continue the conversation. They make you feel like whatever you have to say is the most interesting and important topic they have heard that day.

Unfortunately, many parents don't apply this method when their teenager is attempting to communicate with them. If this happens over a sustained period of time, the teenager begins to realize that talking with their parents about important things is a waste of time. As a result, they turn to friends and people outside the family who will listen to them because they don't feel their parents really care about their problems or what they have to say.

I spend a great deal of time on Facebook, probably too much time. I have almost 2,000 friends on my Facebook page and over 1,000 fans on the Jungle Survival Drivers Training fan page. Most of these friends and fans are my students and their parents. It may sound like I'm bragging and maybe I am, a little. RaRa JuMa is my name on Facebook, and I have a lot of Jungle friends there that I keep in touch with. (Join me in the Jungle and friend me!)

It's important I have the ability to stay in touch with my students. I use my Facebook to monitor if my students are continuing to drive *The Jungle Way* long after they leave Jungle. At any given time while I'm on Facebook, several of my students will want to chat with me when they are online, they will post to my wall various questions, or they express thanks for helping them pass their road test and saving their lives. In many cases, they will ask my advice over topics having nothing to do with driving a car. Let me share one such story that relates back to the communication issue some teens have from time to time with their parents.

I happened to be on Facebook one evening when one of my students wanted to discuss a situation with me. You have to remember, I don't type very fast with my two index fingers, and considering the left index finger is partially amputated, it makes it even more difficult to keep up with my Facebook savvy students. On this evening, it happened to be a young lady, and she was very upset with a situation involving her girlfriends and wanted my advice. She said she felt like an outcast with her friends because all they wanted to do was have sex with boys and drink and use drugs. She wanted badly to be part of the group, but knew how harmful participating in such things would be to her and her family.

I responded by saying to her that I didn't think she was a follower, but a leader. She said she wasn't a follower, but she didn't want to be an outcast from her friends. I explained to her that it sounded to me like she needed to find some new friends. There were plenty of teenagers out there that believed like she did and she just needed to find out who they were and become their friends.

I asked her why she didn't discuss this situation with her parents, and she said it would be embarrassing to discuss it with them and they wouldn't understand anyway. It was good for her to be able to talk with someone other than her parents whom she respected and could trust. I wondered how long she had felt this way about her parents and if the parents had any idea that their level of communication with their daughter had fallen to such a level.

A couple of days passed, and while on Facebook one evening I heard from the young lady again. She was very happy and told me that I was right and she had become friends with some other girls who did believe as she did and she was very grateful for my advice and guidance.

This Facebook encounter made me wonder how many times my children as they were growing up felt that my wife and I wouldn't listen to them and they went to others for advice on such important matters.

Life is pretty fast-paced, and sometimes we just have to slow down and take an inventory of what is really important. We don't get a second chance to raise our kids all over again. We need to make sure we get it right the first time because the mistakes we make will have an impact for a lifetime.

# Chapter 15

## Distractions

Whenever I was involved in an auto accident investigation, I would find out very quickly that a high degree of organization and patience were crucial to conducting a professional investigation. The amount of information that needed to be gathered and processed sometimes seemed, at times, like an overwhelming task. In order to simplify the investigation, it was more efficient if I divided the process into three phases.

The three phases I utilized were "the pre-crash," "the crash," and "the post-crash." It was a simplified approach to segmenting the vast amounts of information, so it would allow me to focus more efficiently. This would result in a more accurate determination of the actual causes of the crash. Kind of like the old adage, "How do you eat an elephant?" And the answer of course would be, "One bite at a time!"

The degree of accuracy was vital to completing the investigation in a timely, efficient, and thorough manner. This was extremely important because many of the investigations would end up in a court setting or if in a unionized work force environment, a grievance panel.

Since the subject of the chapter is distractions, let's focus our attention on distractions and the driver. The reason for the brief introduction regarding the process I used to investigate auto accidents is this. In the pre-crash phase of the investigation, my goal is to create a personality profile of the operators of the vehicle or vehicles involved in the crash. This would enable me to determine their mental state prior to the crash and ultimately help determine the causations and ultimately, the level of fault.

It wasn't always an exact science but in most cases, I was able to pinpoint the primary reasons for the causes of the actual crash. Based on this approach I usually found that distractions were the primary factor that caused the actual crash. I was able to divide these distractions into two separate categories, internal and external distractions. Some of the distractions present leading up to the crash were controllable, and some were not controllable.

In this fast paced world we live in, we all lead pretty busy and active lives. We sometimes move at such a pace that we can't consistently maintain a high degree of focus and patience. Our stress levels, although different for each of us, all have a ceiling as to what we can endure. It's usually called our "breaking point!"

My "breaking point" is different than yours, and yours is different than the next person's. But, we all have one and when we reach it, the result is always the same. We start screwing up, and the number and severity of the mistakes we make as a result increases in direct proportion to our level of frustration or anger.

The problem is, however, that distractions can be very dangerous to the driver. Distractions in driving degrade safety and are a sure recipe for disaster *if* we let them take away our focus. To illustrate this point, I once did a non-scientific experiment with some teen drivers I had after the classroom session ended. I set up the game *Grand Theft Auto* on a television set and had purchased a simulator steering wheel, brake, and accelerator device. The reason I chose this particular driving game was it had meaning. I thought…distractions *steal* your focus as a driver, the real theft involved in driving, and I wanted to prove my point with the teens in a game they could all relate to and many had played before.

I let each student begin, then I slowly added distractions…first, a cell phone call; then I cranked up the radio. A car horn noise blared; then I asked the drivers to continue driving and try to text their mom or dad and type "I love you" to them. Then I gave them driving instructions: stop at the red light ahead; then while there I asked them to place a cell call; then while they were dialing I said, "Stale green light, shadow your brake, look and see left, right, left, right, and check you center mirror, and proceed through the intersection." Every student who participated in the exercise failed miserably. Some of them immediately gave up or became very frustrated and angry.

The more competitive students tried in vain to successfully complete the exercise, but to no avail.

Various studies have shown that multi-tasking is a very ineffective process that people utilize in order to get more things done in a shorter period of time. I have always liked to relate the process of multi-tasking to a person who attempts to juggle several balls at one time, the balls obviously relating to the number of tasks they are trying to complete in certain amount of time. Some people can only juggle one ball at a time and they can do quite well with the one ball, but when they attempt to juggle two or three balls, they usually drop them. They usually give up and move on to something else that is a little easier and less frustrating to master.

These same studies also showed when an individual focuses on one task and one task only, they usually complete the task with a much higher level of competence and quality. When attempting several tasks at one time, they may or may not even complete all the tasks; if they do, the level of competence and quality are usually unacceptable and in many cases they fail completely.

Unfortunately for many wild animals in the highway Jungle, driving a vehicle is the ultimate in multi-tasking, and we already know that multi-tasking is not an effective approach to success. Remember this fact: The average driver makes thirty driving decisions per minute, and for every 500 decisions they make at least one mistake. This mistake might go totally unrecognized or turn into a close call where not enough things go wrong at the right time to cause a collision. Ultimately, if enough mistakes are made, the result could be an auto accident. This mistake ratio increases drastically as you become more distracted while driving.

## Internal and External Distractions

I think you would agree that pretty much every segment of our society is sitting behind the wheel of a motor vehicle at any given time of the day or night. Most of these people honestly feel they are good drivers and usually believe that it's the other drivers in the Jungle that drive like wild animals, not them. So let's spend some time trying to identify who these other drivers are, whoever they may be! Let's also pinpoint some of the distractions we all may encounter as animals in the highway Jungle.

An important aspect of *The Jungle Way* of driving is to provide the parents with the proper training so they will be more confident and effective at teaching and holding their teenage driver accountable for driving *The Jungle Way* after they leave Jungle. In addition, they won't inadvertently contradict *The Jungle Way* as they continue the training process! The first phase of parent training begins with the Jungle Parent Training Class, which is conducted prior to their teen's first day of class.

Whenever I conduct a Parent Training Class I always make an effort, with the help of the parents, to identify who exactly the wild animals are in the highway Jungle and what type of distractions they may experience while driving.

I always explain to them that there are eight sides to a vehicle and I ask them what they are. Since no one has ever come up with the right answer, I will end the suspense for you. There are eight sides to a vehicle: front, rear, left, right, top, bottom, inside the vehicle, and lastly, inside your head. What you are thinking and your attitude at the time is a very important aspect of how effectively you drive. I know I may risk overstating this, but "attitude" plays such an important role in driver safety.

In order to illustrate the degree of distractions an individual driver may face at any time, I like to ask the parents during the training session the following questions. I affectionately call them my 63 Do You's? (E) = External Distractions (I) = Internal Distractions

1.    Do you think you are a good driver? (I) Answer: Yes, in most cases.

2.    Do you feel your initial driver training experience provided you with the skills you needed to become a good driver? (I) Answer: No, I learned from experience.

3.    Do you agree that much of how you drive was learned when you were a beginning driver observing how other people drove? (I) Answer: Somewhat.

4.　　Do you tailgate or as we say in Jungle, Butt Sniff? (I) Answer: No

5.　　Do you know what the correct following distance should be when following another vehicle in traffic? (I) Answer: One car length for every 10 mph. (Inaccurate response. Correct response should be 4 to 6 seconds following distance under 30 mph and 6 to 8 seconds following distance over 30 mph if driving *The Jungle Way*.)

< 30 mph = 4-6 seconds following distance

> 30 mph = 6-8 seconds following distance

6.　　Do you drive with one car length for every 10 mph? (I) Answer: No.

7.　　Do you make complete stops at stop signs? (I) Yes, most of the time, except when I'm in a hurry, or behind schedule.

8.　　Do you make a complete stop before turning right on a red traffic light? (I) Yes, most of the time unless I'm in a hurry, or late for an appointment.

9. Do you think it's possible to get to where you're going quicker by driving faster in city traffic? (I) Answer: Yes.

10. Do you feel that driving faster than the posted speed limit is safe? (I) Answer: Yes, if you're only going 5 to 10 mph over.

11. Do you make proper, safe and legal lane changes? (I) Answer: Yes.

12. Do you know what the correct methods are for making a proper, safe and legal lane change? (I) Answer: Not sure, maybe not.

13. Do you ever exceed the speed limit by 5 to 15 mph or more? (I) Answer: Yes.

14. Do you or have you ever-consumed alcohol before driving a motor vehicle? (I) Answer: Yes.

15. Do you or have you ever had a close call while driving? (I) Answer: Yes.

16. Do you text on your cell phone while driving? (E) Answer: Not very much.

17. Do you talk on your cell phone with either a hands free or regular cell phone? (E) (I) Answer: Yes

18. Do you eat or drink anything while driving? (E) Answer: Yes.

19. Do you listen to the radio or play music while driving? (E) Answer: Yes.

20.    Do you ever get sleepy while driving a vehicle? (I) Answer: Yes.

21.    Do you stop and rest when falling asleep behind the wheel? (I) Answer: No.

22.    Do you ever get angry, or frustrated with other animals on the road? (I) Answer: Yes.

23.    Do you drive with proper hand placement on the steering wheel? (I) Answer: No.

24.    Do you ever drive while you are angry? (I) Answer: Yes.

25.    Do you ever drive when you are hungry? (I) Answer: Yes.

26.    Do you drive when you are worried, stressed, or depressed? (I) Answer: Yes.

27.    Do you ever drive when you don't feel well? (I) Answer: Yes.

28.    Do you ever drive and daydream? (I) Answer: Yes.

29.    Do you ever drive with overconfidence? (I) Answer: I suppose.

30.    Do you ever get lost while driving? (E) (I) Answer: Once in a while.

31.    Do you, if you smoke, do so while driving? (E) (I) Answer: Yes, if a smoker.

32.     Do you or have you ever cried while driving? (E) (I) Answer: Some have and some haven't.

33.     Do you ever use your rearview mirror when backing up? (E) Answer: Of Course.

34.     Do you ever use your cell phone while backing up? (E) (I) Answer: Yes.

35.     Do you ever read while driving" (E) (I) Answer: Yes.

36.     Do you ever use your visor mirror while driving? (E) Answer: Yes.

37.     Do you ever shave while driving? (E) Answer: No, but I've seen people do it.

38.     Do you ever floss while driving? (E) Answer: No, but I've seen others floss.

39.     Do you ever brush your teeth while driving? (E) Answer: No, but I've seen others do it.

40.     Do you ever put on makeup while you are driving? (E) Answer: Yes, if answered by a women.

41.     Do you ever change clothing while driving? (E) Answer: No, but I've heard of people doing so.

42.     Do you ever engage in inappropriate type behavior in a vehicle while driving? (E) (I) Answer: In younger years.

43.     Do you or your passengers ever sing or attempt to dance while driving? (E) Answer: Sometimes.

44.    Do you or your passengers ever attempt to play a musical instrument while driving? (E) Answer: Passengers.

45.    Do you ever try to simulate playing an imaginary musical instrument while driving? (E) Answer: Yes, when I'm happy and in a good mood.

46.    Do you ever drive with your pet or pets in your lap? (E) Answer: No, but I've seen others do it.

47.    Do you ever use any drugs or sleep aids when driving? (I) Answer: No.

48.    Do you ever-complete paperwork while driving? (E) (I) Answer: I have from time to time.

49.    Do you ever use a computer while driving? (E) (I) Answer: I have from time to time.

50.    Do you ever watch DVD's while driving? (E) (I) Answer: No.

51.    Do you ever comb or brush your hair while driving? (E) Answer: Yes.

52.    Do you ever drive without wearing clothing? (E) (I) Answer: No, but I imagine that people have.

53.    Do you ever stare at other vehicles while driving? (E) Answer: Sometimes.

54.    Do you ever look at the scenery while driving? (E) Answer: Sometimes.

55.    Do you ever clean your glasses while driving? (E) Answer: Sometimes.

56.    Do you ever remove or put your contacts in while driving (E) Answer: Sometimes.

57.    Do you ever have anyone sit in your lap while driving? (E) (I) Answer: No.

58.    Do you ever cough or sneeze while driving (E) (I) Answer: Yes, doesn't everyone?

59.    Do you ever hiccup while driving (I) Answer: I have.

60.    Do you drive with your knees? (E) Answer: No, but I know people who do.

61.    Do you ever clean your nose out while driving? (E) Answer: Yes.

62.    Do you ever trim your fingernails while driving? (E) Answer: No.

63.    Do you ever clean your ears while driving? (E) Answer: I have, but not on a regular basis.

So, what do all of these questions and responses really mean to us as we consider our attitudes toward driving and how that affects our safety? Let me clarify the results.

The responses are fairly predictable since everyone thinks he or she is such a good driver and it's always someone else that does such stupid things behind the wheel. Most of my parents won't admit to doing anything wrong while in their vehicle as they are poking their spouse in the ribs, or looking at them with a smile of superiority. This is very normal when you are working with Hyenas and Wild Dogs! It's always the other animal that's the bad or crazy driver, but never them!

The serious side of distracted driving is an ugly picture. The plain and simple fact is distracted driving kills and injures thousands of people every year and this will never change. Unfortunately, most drivers give about as much thought to driving a vehicle correctly as they would give about brushing their teeth. Countless studies have been performed in order to prove the fact that distracted driving is one of the primary causes of auto accidents and the resulting deaths and injuries.

**The "BIG FIVE" Ways to Kill Yourself in a Vehicle.**

Distraction takes a whole different level when we talk about the "BIG FIVE". I know this may seem harsh, but these are deadly reasons that do not mix with *any* type of driver: teen or adult. The analogy of "the Big Five" animals that people seek to see when on a Jungle safari is used because I want you to remember this – if you negate the dangers of these 5, you minimize your driving safety risks and improve safety, it is just that simple. I say deadly because I mean deadly, these can and *will* kill teen drivers. These are the top five dangerous elements added to driving that I want to stress as absolutely things which should not

be combined with driving at any time.

1. **Alcohol** – The statistics are sobering, whether you want to hear them or believe them, the potential for an accident and resulting death and injuries is startling. M.A.D.D. (Mother's Against Drunk Driving) claims in a recent finding that car crashes are the leading cause of death among teenagers, and 1/3 of those deaths are alcohol related. One in five teens binge drink and only 1 in 100 parents believe it. Unfortunately, drinking has become a major consideration that has to be addressed.

2. **Drugs** – illegal or legal prescription drugs. Although one may not believe the statistics, this factor plays a role in our teen society more than we would like to admit. Drugs are as dangerous, if not potentially more dangerous than alcohol because they impair judgment and one's ability in making driving decisions instantly and with great effect.

3. **Cell phone use and Texting** – These two are a sign of the era in which we live today, becoming so commonplace in our society that they have to be address as potential hazards. Bottom line – a distracted teen driver with a cell hone (calling or texting) is a dangerous driver. According to a report from The Community Traffic Safety Coalition, drivers distracted by cell phones are as effectively impaired as a drunk driver with a BAC of .08, startling statistics.

4. **Speed** – The average driver goes 5-15 mph over the speed limit. Speed kills, and if you can control your speed, you can control your safety. Speed combined with

inexperience and multi-tasking (distracted driving) inside the car is a deadly combination for teens.

5. **Distraction** inside the car. A distracted, inexperience teen driver is a formula for disaster. Let's talk about the 2 of the 3 areas of space that you as a driver have direct control over. Those two areas are the space inside the car and the inside of your head (your attitude). Interestingly, these two elements are with each teen inside the car each time they drive. Add friends to the mix, and three categories of external distractions that affect all drivers, especially teen drivers: 1. lights, 2. sound, and 3. movement, and in addition you have the broad spectrum of internal distractions.

The use of alcohol, drugs, cell phones, lack of sleep, and anger are the most publicized forms of distractions while operating a motor vehicle. Most recently, texting or using cell phones while driving has captured the attention of the media and various state and federal governmental agencies. Several states have passed laws restricting or banning the use of cell phones and texting while driving. Many states are proposing new laws that would ban or restrict cell phone usage of any kind while driving a vehicle.

Passing laws will help reduce the number of distracted driving related accidents, but those laws will never eliminate the problem. As long as human beings operate motor vehicles there will be distracted drivers. In addition to laws that restrict or attempt to control the driving behavior of people, there needs to be a greater emphasis placed on parents of teenage drivers.

Parents must take an active role in educating and holding their teen accountable for driving with the right attitude. This attitude is one where teens learn they must drive for everybody in their car and everyone else on the road, in other words, they must be inspired to drive with courtesy, patience, and concern for others. Parents must set this example and become driving role models for their teen.

As I have stated previously, it has been proven beyond any doubt that teens will emulate the way their parents drive and the things they do while driving. Always remember THE BIG FIVE, and please don't bring them with you into the automobile. (i.e. – control the space *within* the vehicle).

The challenge to every teen driver is to survive – by using *The Jungle Way*, utilizing the concepts, and applying them every time you take to the road in an automobile.

The challenge of parents is keeping our future from dying on our nation's highways, and is in the hands of each and every parent who allows their teenager to drive.

# Chapter 16

## Frustrations

I wasn't planning on writing a chapter on frustrations, but I'm left with no other choice after today. It's either write about it or I'm going to go crazy! Let me explain.

One of the unique aspects of Jungle Survival Drivers Training is the life-long commitment we make to each of our students. We will drive with a student for as long as they want for any reason at no additional cost. It may be because they were scared due to a close call they experienced; maybe they were involved in an auto accident, maybe they would like to learn how to drive in winter weather, maybe they are having a negative experience driving with their parents or the parents are having a negative experience driving with their teen, or for any other reason they can think of.

As a result of our commitment, I spend most of my weekends driving with students and parents who need additional training. On a Saturday on one such weekend, I performed a drive and I'm still upset and confused over what transpired. The story illustrates the confusion a lot of teenagers have in the process of learning to drive.

# "I Can't Tell You Because He Will Get Angry"

First of all, when I am asked to drive with a student who has graduated from Jungle, but is struggling with their driving skills, I always request that one or both of the parents ride along with their teen. I ask this in order to follow up with my efforts to instruct the parents on *The Jungle Way* of teaching their teens to drive.

On this particular day, I was greeted at Jungle by a father and his daughter Heather, and even though I always know the purpose of the drive, I ask the teen why they think their parents want me to drive with them. Their response always amazes me because it never matches the reason the parents had previously explained to me when they made the appointment to drive. Oh, by the way, when the parents call to set up the ride, we always explain to them that they are required to ride along with their teen and me.

Well, on this day I asked Heather why she thought her parents wanted me to drive with her and she responded with, "I haven't driven a car since I graduated from Jungle over a year ago!" I asked her why, and her father said they haven't been able to drive with her because they spent their time driving with her older brother and didn't have time for her. I asked the father if he would be riding along with us and he indicated that he was not going to go with us and gave no particular reason. Depending on the mood I'm in at the time, I would usually challenge the parent but in this

case I decided to focus my attention on Heather and we walked out to the car to begin our drive.

Even though it had been over a year since Heather had graduated from Jungle, I remembered her very well. Heather was a little obsessive compulsive by nature and therefore, fearful of driving. She gave me the reason for wanting to drive at this time because all her friends had gotten their license she felt it was time she got hers.

As we began the drive, I could tell immediately that Heather had forgotten most of what we had taught her a year earlier, so I had to treat her like a brand new driver. She was both nervous and scared at the same time, so I spent the first half hour providing encouragement while refreshing her memory as to *The Jungle Way* of driving. After a period of time she began to relax, and then out of the clear blue she asked me if I heard about the accident.

I said, "What accident?"

She said, "The one on Monday."

She explained to me that someone she knew from school lost control of his car and went off the road and hit a pole and a tree. She informed me that there were no injuries, but he totaled his mother's brand new car!

I asked her if he was a Jungle graduate and she told me that he was. I then asked her his name, but she refused my request because she felt he would get angry if he found out who told me. I explained to her the importance of my knowing who he was because I wanted to call his parents and schedule a time to perform an accident investigation and a follow-up drive with them and the young man. This is an important aspect of *The Jungle Way*. It helps us to keep our kids from repeating the same mistakes. I told her he was obviously going too fast for conditions and lost control of the car as a result. He could have very easily been seriously injured or killed! She repeated again that she couldn't tell me who he was, but she did say that he was her former boyfriend.

By this time, I was becoming very frustrated and in a last attempt to convince her to tell me who he was, I used the guilt trip approach with her. I asked her how she would feel if at some point in the future he had another accident and he was injured or killed. She smiled at me and said confidently, "He's not going to get killed in a car accident." It was very evident that she was interpreting my concern as that of an overreacting parent.

I should have let the whole thing go because, after all, I was supposed to be focusing on her driving issues and not her former boyfriend having an accident, but I couldn't. I realized her lack of cooperation and understanding was beginning to make me angry. I decided to temporarily let it go, so I could focus on her and her driving problems.

Whenever I complete a follow-up drive with a student, I always review the results of the drive with the parent. After Heather finished parking the car, her father approached the car with a smile on his face. It was obvious he was anxious for me to let him know what I thought about her driving. I reviewed with him the obvious fact that she had forgotten most of what I taught her the previous year and that she was a very timid and nervous driver. I wanted to schedule some additional drives with Heather and him so we could get her to where she needed to be. I indicated that if he would like we could go inside the Jungle and schedule some future drive times with him and Heather. His expression almost turned to a look of panic, and he said he would wait until he had his calendar in front of him before he would schedule anything. You have to remember that as part of the Jungle commitment, we drive forever for no charge. Despite this fact, most of the time I have to convince the parents to let me drive with their teen.

At this point, I shared with Heather's father my concern and frustration and the request I made of Heather to divulge the name of the young man involved in the accident. He just looked at her and smiled. He recommended that maybe they could invite him to come with her as part of her next driving practice with me. I wasn't happy with his reaction to my dilemma, so I asked him directly if he could let me know who the young man was. He just smiled at his daughter as she nervously smiled back and said they had to leave. I asked him to call me on the following Monday to arrange some additional drives and he said he would, thanked me, and left with Heather. I walked back to Jungle just muttering to myself, "Unbelievable. Unbelievable." And just before I entered the building I actually yelled out, "Unbelievable!" I never heard from them again. Seriously, that is unbelievable.

Since I named this chapter "Frustrations," I might as well share the story I mentioned earlier in the book about never becoming too proud of what you've accomplished because if tragedy strikes, accomplishments will seem meaningless.

## "The Dread of a Flashing Red"

It was 1:00 A.M. on a Friday night, and I was on Facebook playing one my favorite games and chatting with some of my former students. I'm a night owl, so when one of my students asked me if I heard about the accident that had happened earlier that night, I informed him that I wasn't aware of any accident. He explained that there was a bad accident at a flashing red and the road had been closed down because they were rerouting traffic. He had to find another way home. As soon as I finished typing my response to him, several other students asked me about the same accident and I indicated to them I had no knowledge of the accident. I also asked if they had heard anything and to please let me know if when did.

The next day, I found out the horrible outcome of the accident because it was all over the news. Based on the reports, at about 11:30 P.M. a car traveling at about 45 mph heading southbound failed to stop at a flashing red light and impacted an eastbound car on the driver side. A nineteen-year-old male who died at the scene of the accident drove the eastbound car. The driver of the southbound car suffered a broken leg and his female passenger suffered minor injuries.

Obviously, this was a very sad and tragic accident which could have been easily avoided by both drivers. It was made even more tragic to me personally because the driver of the car which had caused the accident was one of my former students. When I found out the particulars of the accident, I decided to let an adequate amount of time pass before I would contact the mother of the young man who caused the accident. I was aware of the fact that he had broken his leg, but I was more concerned over the emotional injuries he had to be suffering from.

After an adequate amount of time had passed, it just so happened that his younger brother, who was also a Jungle graduate, had enrolled in a follow-up training class at Jungle, which was being conducted at the time. After asking him how his brother was doing, I requested that he ask his mother if I could conduct an accident investigation drive with his brother and her. The next day he told me that his mother thought it would be a great idea if I would drive with her and her son but unfortunately, after his broken leg healed, he had moved out of the house and they had no idea where he was staying.

I found this rather odd, and since I knew what high school he was attending, I asked some of my students if they had seen him at school. They indicated that he was attending classes and he seemed to be doing okay. I had been told that he attended the funeral of the young man who had died. The mother of the young man told him not to blame himself for the death of her son because God had decided He had another purpose for him and that it was time to take him to heaven. They had nineteen wonderful years with him and they were happy for that. I was also told later that my student had asked if he could visit the funeral site to pray for the young man, and he was granted permission to do so.

In my efforts to contact my student, I have tried everything I could think of and at the time of this writing I have been unsuccessful with my efforts. I hope he is doing well and coping with the tragedy that has forever changed his life and the lives of others. I continually hope and pray for this young man and his family and for the family of the young man whose life was taken. I will continue in my efforts to contact him.

# Chapter 17

## Never Let the Wheels Spin

Winter driving is always a challenge. My company was founded in Michigan, and we know what winter is every year. I believe it makes a teenager a better driver. One of the most terrifying moments in anyone's driving life is when they lose control of their vehicle as a result of a skid. It happens so quickly that it's over before you know what happened. Most people blame their loss of control on the infamous "black ice." (You know…that mysterious frozen substance that hides in waiting for the unsuspecting, innocent, and no doubt, good driver! Besides, it's always a great excuse when your friends ask you why you're driving a different vehicle. All you have to do is tell them your "black ice" story, and they will be immediately sympathetic because it's probably happened to them.)

Jungle drivers don't believe in "black ice!" They know if the temperature is below freezing and there is moisture around, or on the pavement, there will be icy spots or patches of ice and they adjust their driving to fit the conditions. They have been taught that there are three main factors which can cause skids: 1) Weather, 2) Speed, and 3) Tires.

The weather conditions change from day to day, hour to hour, and minute to minute. Jungle drivers know the importance of always having good tires with proper tread depth and tire pressure. They know that good tires are vital to maintaining rolling traction with the road.

They also realize that there are four phases of a skid: a. A rolling wheel, b. A spinning wheel, c. A sliding wheel, and d. An all-wheel skid. They know the key to not losing control of their vehicle is that they must drive in direct proportion to loss of traction. This simply means that as the weather and road conditions change, they must be proactive and slow down so their wheels don't spin. They apply this skid control philosophy when starting up from a stopped position; slowing down sooner while approaching stopped vehicles, traffic lights and stop signs; making a turn; or prior to entering a curve.

Sometimes the loss of traction conditions might require them to drive significantly below the speed limit while drastically increasing their following distance. Normally, Jungle drivers maintain a four to six second following distance when traveling under 30 mph, and six to eight seconds when traveling over 30 mph. As traction decreases, the following distance is increased to eight to twelve seconds or more.

< 30 mph = 4-6 seconds following distance

> 30 mph = 6-8 seconds following distance

Many of the newer cars are equipped with various technologies like Electronic Stability Control. This is a technology that improves the ability of the vehicle to control, or prevent skidding situations by limiting the spinning of the wheels during loss of traction situations. Depending on the vehicle manufacturer, the technology can be turned on or off depending on the driving conditions.

If your vehicle isn't equipped with this technology, you can utilize the vehicle's tachometer to prevent your wheels from spinning and transitioning into a skid. The tachometer measures RPMs, or revolutions per minute, that a vehicle's engine is turning over to provide power to the wheels. The tachometer sort of looks like the speedometer, but instead of miles or kilometers per hour, it will have the numbers from one to eight or nine, depending on the size of the engine. Most vehicles operate in a range between 1,500 and 3,000 RPMs as they are moving down the road.

When driving in weather conditions where there is loss of traction, just before the vehicle begins its slide, the tires will began to spin because they are losing rolling traction with the surface of the road. As this spinning action occurs, the tachometer will begin to spike as the wheels spin faster due to loss of rolling traction. This spinning action causes the engine to race and the tachometer will show the increase in the RPMs the engine is producing. When this happens, immediately get off the gas and the vehicle will slow itself down. The tachometer needle will drop and then level off at the speed where the wheels have regained rolling traction. This is the speed you should be driving at based on the existing conditions and available traction. This process is defined as driving in direct proportion to loss of traction.

Keeping your vehicle under control in a skidding situation is a very challenging and difficult process. Once a wheel starts to spin, you usually have just a fraction of a second from the beginning of a skid to when the wheels start to slide. Just remember that a sliding wheel will always pick up momentum, and a sliding wheel will always travel faster than a rolling wheel and will try to catch up and lead the rolling wheels. So, when the back end of your vehicle begins to slide to the left or right by just fifteen to twenty degrees, your vehicle is already reached the point of an out-of-control four wheel skid, which means it is too late to recover.

Most people have learned over the years that in order to control a skidding car, you should always steer in the direction of the skid or where you want your car to go. Therefore, if the car is skidding to the right, steering to the right will decrease the skid, and if it skids to the left, steering to the left will help to slow the skid. You might

have to make a few steering adjustments to get the car straight; and then once the car is straight, you firmly apply the brake.

When explained, this sounds like a simple process which can be easily executed by an experienced driver, but this is usually not the case. The faster you are traveling the faster the car slides, and in many cases, the car has already traveled passed fifteen to twenty degrees. At this point most people panic and apply the brakes. This can be a fatal mistake because the brake should never be applied unless the vehicle is under control and the car is traveling straight. Once at an angle when the brakes are applied, the front end, being heavier, acts like a fulcrum point, and the back end of the car whips around the front end. Remember, a sliding wheel always travels faster than a rolling wheel. This panic reaction leads to an all-wheel skid, which I call a "close-your-eyes-hold-on-and-pray-to-God-you-don't-die skid."

Driving in direct proportion to loss of traction, which I explained earlier, can prevent the majority, if not all, of these skidding situations. If you happen to have ABS (automatic brake system) brakes or anti-lock brakes on your vehicle (which is a great technology that work well if properly used), you still have to get your vehicle straight before you brake!

Many experienced drivers were taught to pump, or stab, their brakes when the feel they are skidding. These techniques work well when traveling at slow speeds and the driver is not in panic mode. But, at higher speeds, it becomes more difficult to use this process due the lack of time available to react properly. ABS brakes work great if you use them properly. Get the car straight first by counter steering, and once straight firmly apply the brakes and hold them down, never pump or stab ABS brakes. If you do, the action will throw you in to a more violent skid. ABS brakes will slow your vehicle down in a controlled safe manner.

At 35 mph on slippery roads, good tires and ABS brakes will bring you to a stop at less than 150 feet and in a straight line. They are a great technology if properly used.

I'm sure you can see how all of this advice is useful to keeping drivers safe in various weather conditions. The most important advice is to make sure to drive at a speed where your wheels don't spin. A spinning wheel is your vehicle telling you that you need to drive slower; it's your early warning system. Teach these techniques to your teenager so they can benefit. Remember, they have to deal with these situations as an inexperienced and distracted teenage driver. Other than doing doughnuts in a parking lot, many of them have never been in a high-speed skidding situation. Teach them the right way so they don't have to know what the wrong way feels like.

# Chapter 18

## The Mind of a Teenage Driver

Wow! "The Mind of a Teenage Driver" is an incredible topic to write about. What a mystery; it seems at times that the word "communication" is a misnomer in the teen driving game. What is inside that complex mind? How do I effectively communicate with the person who has that mind? What does a 61-year-old man know about the mind of a teenager? I was actually asked this question by one of my students the other day. I was proudly announcing to the class that I have been writing a book and the last chapter I had finished was entitled, "Does Anyone Here Speak Teenager?" One of my students looked almost glaringly at me and politely raised her hand and said, "What do you know about the mind of a teenager? You're old!" I realized then it was all about communication.

After being caught off-balance for a brief moment, I collected my thoughts, swallowed hard, and thought for a moment as the entire class waited for my response. I finally said, "That's a very good question. What *does* an old guy like me know about teenagers? Well, let's see. I was a teenager once." Her response was an obvious one: "That was in the old days!" I replied with, "You know, I raised three teenagers and they turned out pretty good, and I have trained over 13,000 teenagers in the last seven years. I also have almost 2,000 Facebook friends to date, and most of them are former students." I asked her how many friends she had on her Facebook and she just smiled and didn't respond. At this point, the rest of the class looked at her and started laughing, and she decided to accept the fact that I just might know a few things about the mind of a teenager.

The mind of a teenager exists in all of us, but as we get older, we have a tendency to forget about how we were as teenagers. Sure, the times were different than today, but we still perceived and reacted to various situations and challenges as teenagers with the same teenage mind. That mind does not change from generation to generation.

Today's teens are still preoccupied with things like, friends, school, who's popular and who's not, and who the nerds, Goths, and emos are. They're concerned about activities ranging from various sports, plays, music, vacations, and sleeping. Once in a while, they even have a little time for a few quality moments with their family. It seems as if they are the busiest people in the world with never enough time to get everything done, and they never do.

The world of today's teenager is vastly different and much faster and hectic than the world of previous generations. Technology has exploded in every area, and teenagers have fully embraced the new toys it has created for them. Their minds have been taken over by iTouches iPods, iPhones, Blackberries, YouTube, Facebook, Twitter, Xbox, Playstation and Wii! They are attached to these devices by electronic umbilical cords that enable them to withdraw into their own inner world whenever they desire to do so, further diminishing their interpersonal and communication skills.

The motivations of teenagers are fairly simple as a rule. Hanging out with friends is probably at the top of their list of fun things to do. Getting good grades in school can be important depending on the environment they are raised in.

Some teenagers will do almost anything in their attempts to please or at the very least, not disappoint their parents. I have asked many of my classes to give me a show of hands if any of them have ever "shared knowledge" (the Jungle term for cheating) in any of their classes. Usually, about 95% of them raise their hands. There are always a couple of students that insist that they would never do such a thing, and the rest of the class laughs and proclaims that they are lying. It's his or her opinion; everybody shares knowledge from time to time.

When asked why they share knowledge their response is always the same: "So I won't get in trouble with my parents by bringing home bad grades," or "To get into a good college." The bad grades part is highly subjective. To some, a bad grade is D or C and to others, anything less than an A is bad.

The motivation by a teen to please their parents has always been present. In many cases the motivation is sincere and teens really want their parents to be proud of them and their success. However, in many cases fear and the resulting punishment and scorn is the primary reason for doing what teens do. The following story illustrates the point.

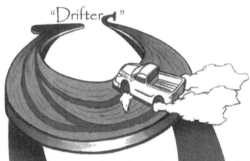

"Drifter"

I was driving with a couple of students the other day, and as we were stopped at an intersection, the driver informed me that she was involved in a pretty serious accident during the past summer. I asked her what happened, and she explained to me that she was a passenger in a pick-up truck driven by a guy from school. He was attempting to demonstrate to her and another girl how to drift around a curve. Drifting is the process where the driver rapidly accelerates the vehicle while moving around a curve. The purpose is to slide the rear wheels to the outside of the curve so the back end of the vehicle moves sideways or drifts around the curve. Drifting originally was made popular from the movie Tokyo Drift. It has since become a popular fad with teenagers, predominately males.

"We were on a gravel road and moving really fast. I was scared to death, and my girlfriend and I were screaming!" I asked her if she participated in the thrill-seeking experience "I was listening to the radio." I asked her again if she participated by encouraging the young man driving. "Well, I guess so, even though I was frightened. It was really exciting."

As she was telling me the story, I noticed that she was actually getting more excited as she continued. Her facial expressions became very animated; she had the look you would see on someone scared to death on a fast roller coaster. Her eyes kept getting wider and wider as her smile broadened. It appeared as though she was actually reliving the accident as we drove down the road. You would have thought that her recounting of the accident would bring back the memories of fear and regret, not thrill and excitement! I had to remind myself that she was a fifteen-year-old teenager!

As she continued with her story she said, "All of a sudden the truck spun around very fast and we crashed into a big tree. We had to crawl out of the truck, which had wrapped itself around the tree. None of us was seriously hurt, just a few bumps and bruises, but the truck was destroyed and it was hauled away on a flat bed trailer.

"We called the police to report the accident. A lady police officer came to the accident scene and asked us what happened. We told her that a deer ran out in front of us and we swerved to avoid hitting it and hit the tree instead. She asked if we needed an ambulance and we told her we were

okay and our parents were on their way to get us. The kid driving was really mad because the police officer gave him a ticket for not keeping his truck under control. The lady officer told him since there wasn't a dead deer, there was no proof the deer caused the accident, so she had to give him the ticket."

I asked her how her dad reacted when she told him how the accident really happened and how long was she grounded as a result of her poor judgment. Her response was, "Oh, he still thinks it was a deer!" All I could do was laugh along with the student in the back seat of our Jungle car.

As I continued her instruction into *The Jungle Way* of driving, I asked her if she realized how fortunate she and her friends were. She realized that they were lucky nothing more serious had happened to them. I told her that was the response I hoped to hear from her. I explained to her that circumstances could have changed the outcome to the point where we wouldn't even be discussing the event because she wouldn't be here as a result of the accident. She nodded her head in agreement and we drove on. She was silent for the rest of the training session, and we never discussed the accident again during the three weeks of the class. I feel strongly that she got the message. I even have the hope that she will someday tell her dad how the accident really happened.

# It's Not Really Cool.

What teenagers say is appropriate while driving a car is not as cool as they think. In many cases distractions inside the car become the primary reason for a teenage driver and their passengers not showing up for school the next day.

One of my students was really in to customizing various aspects of his car. He loved everything about cars. How they look, how fast they can go, and what you can do to "trick them out." As a matter of fact, I have often spoken with him about making car-customizing his career someday. He has a very strong mechanical and creative ability that would help him to be successful if he chose to pursue such a career. He had previously graduated from Jungle a couple of years earlier and has become a permanent fixture of Jungle and visits quite often. He also likes to drive fast, very fast in his little white sports car. Unfortunately, his need for speed caught up with him last year. He was stopped by a state trooper and ticketed for driving 101 mph on a street with a posted speed limit of 55 mph!

When he got home he told his mother of the incident. As you might expect, she was very upset. Her son's explanation for speeding was due to the fact that he felt sick and thought he was going to throw up. He didn't want to throw up in his car, so he was trying to get home as quickly as possible and be sick there.

His mother obviously wasn't moved by his plight, so she decided to suspend his driving privileges for a period of time in an attempt to correct his speeding problem. Suspension of driving privileges never corrects a teenager's need for speed attitude. Unfortunately, the level of a teenager's immaturity and lack of frontal lobe development prevents any form of consistent rational thinking.

I happened to find out about the speeding ticket when I was helping one of my students prepare for his road test. It just so happened that the teen who was stopped for speeding was his best friend. He told me the entire story and I later called the mother of the speeding student to find out the real story.

She was so upset that she was actually crying on the phone. I asked her if I could meet with her and her son to discuss the incident. We agreed to meet on a Sunday, which happened to be the same time that Michigan State University was playing in the Final Four in Detroit. Since I graduated from Michigan State, and I am a loyal and fanatic supporter of my school, it was a difficult decision to schedule a meeting at such a time, but my students and their families come first, even over my Spartans.

The meeting was rather emotional with the mother sobbing the entire time. My goal with her son was to determine if he had any remorse over his actions that had so upset his mother. He appeared to be somewhat sincere in his commitment to never do such a foolish thing again.

We talked for over an hour and reached an agreement that he would not be able to drive his car again until he completed a research paper on teen driving accidents, which he would submit to me for my grade and approval. In addition, he would be required to drive with me for a period of time deemed necessary by me to demonstrate his renewed commitment to drive *The Jungle Way*.

We drove several times over the next few weeks, and he consistently drove *The Jungle Way*. He submitted his research paper for my review, and I found it to be an outstanding effort on his part. He convinced me that he had seen the light and would never do something so foolish in the future. I told him that I had spies everywhere and if he ever drove fast again, I would know. A year later, he is still driving *The Jungle Way*. He stops by every couple weeks to see if I've received any reports from my spy network about him. I just smile and tell him to keep up to the good work!

## What Eardrums?!

This young man is actually fairly typical of a young male teenage driver. He showed up the other day to demonstrate the new stereo system he had purchased and installed. He was so proud of the fact that the subwoofer produced over 4,000 watts of power, and if he turned it up full blast, it could vibrate the windows on a house a block away, not to mention every loose part on the car!

He asked me if I wanted to take a ride with him, so I could experience his new system. I agreed and we headed out on the road. I told him not to turn it up full blast because I valued my eardrums. He laughed and said he would only play the music at the lowest level. You have to understand that I'm a very open-minded individual and love it when my students want to share their experiences with me.

As we proceeded on our journey, he turned on the stereo system he had painstakingly installed in his car. He was so proud that his face beamed with excitement as he slowly cranked up the volume to the lowest level. Let me tell you something. A teen's lowest level is not the same as my lowest level! Just a split second before my eardrums were about to explode, I yelled for him to turn it off! Seriously, I couldn't believe the pain in my ears. They actually ached and throbbed for several minutes after the system was turned off.

He apologized to me and explained that it takes awhile to build up a tolerance for the various sound levels. I asked him if those tolerances were reached as a result of a person going deaf! He just laughed as we headed back to the Jungle.

This story represents just a glimpse of what teenagers think are fun and exciting things to do while driving or being a passenger in a car. As far as a teenager is concerned, just about anything goes because they don't really take the time to think or imagine what could happen to any of them if things go wrong!

Remember, we were all teenagers once upon a time. Think of the things we did in a car, things that we got away with because nothing bad ever happened. No one was injured or killed, there wasn't any damage, and no one got into trouble because our parents never found out what crazy things we did even though they did the same crazy things. They worried for us, though, because of what they use to do, and that is why we worry when our kids began to drive by themselves, or with friends in the car with them. Will they do what we did or maybe even worse?

## *The Jungle Way* is the Cool Way to Drive

Having raised three children over the years, I realized early on that what I thought was important for them to learn was far from what they felt was important. Three teens provided me with a real-world basis to experiment and prove *The Jungle Way*. When it comes to learning to drive a car their motivations, expectations, and perceptions are vastly different than that of an adult.

Some teens take drivers training for a variety of reasons. Their friends are doing it, their parents think it's time, or they think it would be cool to drive a car and not have to rely on their parents to haul them around. For others, they are intimidated and even afraid by even the mere thought of driving a car. They do realize that driving a car is a necessary part of life, and they might as well get it over with.

# Chapter 19

## Taming the Wild Dog

*The Jungle Way* of driving is unique in many ways, and as explained earlier in the book, the association with the human animal and how they drive is one such way that uniqueness is displayed. As I like to say, "It's a Jungle Thing" to my students. Good skills and practices become habits. There are many different animals in the highway Jungle as explained in Chapter 1. One such animal is the Wild Dog! The Jungle definition of a Wild Dog is "drivers who take a lot of risky chances, drive over the speed limit, roll through right turns on reds and stop signs, they don't signal while making lane changes, charge red lights and stale green lights, eat and drink, and they drive 10 to 15 mph or more over the speed limit. No matter how fast the flow of traffic is moving, it's never moving fast enough for them. They always think the faster they go the sooner they will get to where they are going. They don't care the least bit what the other animals on the road think. They are so bold and over confident that they will admit they're bad drivers and are proud of all the things they do wrong. Only the most skilled Jungle Trainers can tame a Wild Dog. Generally there is not much hope for them." Don't critique a Wild Dog's driving because they will just tell you they can drive the way they do because God gave them extra quick reflexes and skills that allow them to do so! They will then tell you that you should never attempt to drive their way because they have had many years of practice. Wild Dogs do provide a benefit to the more responsible drivers on the road. Many times it is possible to learn from the bad examples of others like the Wild Dog. The following story, "Taming the Wild Dog," can better illustrate what defines a Wild Dog behind the wheel and how we can all learn from what others do wrong.

There is nothing more rewarding than the look on a teenage driver's face when the lights come on because they learned something important and exciting for the first time. It's the moment when they finally see it and get it! One of my favorite training techniques is to take my students out onto the highway Jungle and teach them how to drive *The Jungle Way* in rush hour traffic. Rush hour traffic is the perfect time to demonstrate how *The Jungle Way* of driving is effective in any type of driving situation.

Any time we embark on a particular training safari we have to establish ahead of time what our goal is. On this safari the goal was to teach and apply the methods of *The Jungle Way*, which allow any driver to move through traffic with total control of the vehicle and their attitude despite the size of the herd around them.

In order to achieve our stated goal on this safari, the students need to gain an understanding of space and attitude and how they work together. Once taught, they come to the realization that in order to control the space through which their vehicle is moving, they must be able to control their attitude. I explain to my students that there are eight sides to a vehicle; the front, rear, right side, left side, the top, underneath, inside the car, and inside your head. They only have control over two of the eight sides, the space in the front of their vehicle and what's going on inside their head, which is their attitude.

As we all know, driving in the highway Jungle is one of the most hazardous activities that any of us participate in on a daily basis. The factors that are responsible for the countless accidents, injuries, and property damage are many and varied. Road rage, in particular, has become one of the more prevalent factors simply because there are an increasing number of vehicles driving in the Jungle and those vehicles are being driven by animals that are more stressed and distracted than ever before.

Teaching Jungle students the proper methods is not as difficult as you may think. Insuring that those methods become long-term driving habits is where the challenge lies. We have an old saying at Jungle, "Thirty days to form a habit, thirty days to save a life." Simply stated, it is impossible to teach a habit. Habits can only be developed through the teaching of the proper methods and by applying and practicing these methods every day for thirty days. As a result, they will become permanent habits. Where does this leave us with our students? Since we only have them for twenty-four hours in the classroom and ten hours behind the wheel, and not for the necessary thirty days, we must rely on the parents to complete the training task. Jungle places a great deal of emphasis on this task. We must provide the parents with the highest level of training and support in order to insure they are successful in their training efforts. They must have a complete understanding of *The Jungle Way* and how to hold their teenagers accountable for driving *The Jungle Way*. I would like to discuss the parent training in more detail, but I have to leave on my rush hour training safari.

Let's begin our safari story, "Taming the Wild Dog." Rush hour traffic is not unlike the chaos of a wild animal stampede where each animal continually reestablishes its position within the out-of-control herd. Many of the animals in the herd are at times on the edge of panic and often display emotions such as fear, anger, frustration, impatience, anxiety, rudeness, and stress to name a few. Driving properly in this type of Jungle environment poses many challenges for a new and inexperienced student driver. *The Jungle Way* teaches students how to effectively travel through such chaos while controlling their emotions and responding effectively to the other animals that can sometimes lose control of their emotions.

On this particular day we were traveling in the part of the highway Jungle called the East Beltline! The Beast was the vehicle of choice on this particular day. The Beast is painted entirely to look like it is morphing into a Bengal Tiger. There is no better test of a teen than the Beast on a busy road!

I have found over the years that most people learn more effectively through observation, especially teenagers with their shorter attention span. In order to accomplish our goal of successfully teaching the students how to drive *The Jungle Way* in rush hour traffic, I decided to incorporate the process of taming a Wild Dog! It is not an easy task, but with the right amount of patience and proper communication, not an impossible one.

Before getting too far ahead of myself, I think it would be appropriate to identify the participants on this particular driving safari. Behind the wheel was a young Jungle trainee named Mark. He was a very personable and bright young man of fifteen. He was a bit overconfident, but still possessing the attitude that he had a great deal to learn. In the back seat and sitting to my left was Chad, and behind me and to my right was Heather. As you can imagine, they were all very nervous and apprehensive about the thought of venturing into the part of the Jungle we were about to visit.

In order to reach the part of the Jungle where I would begin my taming lesson, we had to travel a short distance on the path called Interstate 96 before exiting onto the East Beltline. It was Mark's first drive on the interstate, but he handled it quite well. As we exited the interstate, there was the typical yellow sign indicating that the recommended speed on the exit was 45 mph. At this point I always explain to my safari participants that this is way too fast for the exit, and they will never make the upcoming curve at such a speed. At this point, I apply my trusty secondary brake to make sure we navigate the turn safely.

At the end of the exit we have to stop at a watering hole (intersection) with a traffic light. I always enjoy our time at this particular watering hole because it presents several challenges and a great deal of excitement for my young trainees. Here we find over a dozen signs and markings that indicate very clearly that they have reached a

227

one-way path and they can only turn right. It never fails; the young drivers always ask, "Which way should I turn?" I always respond with, "Hey, just this one time let's turn left for a quick thrill!" I say this jokingly, of course, and with my left foot I firmly press down on my secondary brake, just in case the young driver takes me seriously. It's at this moment I point out to the driver the signs and markings that indicate a right turn only. We always have a good laugh over this obvious lack of awareness.

This particular traffic light is a very short one due to the heavy movement of animals up and down the East Beltline, so it's usually red. Since there are two right turn lanes, I usually have my students position themselves in the right lane closest to the curb because it's easier for them to complete the turn. While we are waiting at the light, I explain to my trainees my plan to tame a Wild Dog. They are somewhat confused at first, but once we start the training process they figure out the purpose pretty quickly.

"Look to our left. See all of those animals stopped at the watering hole on the other side of the expressway? After we turn right, the next light will be red and we are going to stop. At that point all of those animals are going to be stampeding up behind us. By the time they get to where we are waiting, the light is going to turn green, and they are going to cut in front of us. I want you to notice that when our light turns green the next two lights at the watering holes ahead of us are going to also be green, but they will turn red prior to the herds behind and in front of us. Due to the fact that many of them are Hyenas and Wild Dogs, they are overly aggressive and aim extremely low in their steering. As a result, they will have to apply their brakes and stop. We will do the opposite by letting up on the gas before the lights change, and by the time we get there, the lights will turn to green and we will be able to continue through both watering holes while we pass all of the other animals who had to stop.

"Now, here's the plan. I'm going to pick out a Wild Dog and show it the errors of its ways." It's at this point that I looked in my side mirror and caught a glimpse of a Wild Dog cutting in and out of traffic behind us as we were approaching the next watering hole. It happened to be a black Porsche Cayenne Turbo. They can reach speeds of over 140 mph and it's an SUV! Why anyone would need such a car is beyond me!

As the Porsche races by us, I explain to my trainees that that is the Wild Dog we are going to train. "Okay guys. Watch. See how he is racing up to the light even though it's stale green? Look. The light is turning red and he slamming on his brakes! Now, when we get to the watering hole, the light is going to turn green. As we pass by him while he is waiting, I want everyone to wave at him." Mark, the driver, became very concerned at this point because he was afraid of making the Wild Dog angry. I explained to him that all we were going to do is wave, so why would he become angry at our gesture of friendship? I told him how much fun it was to have another animal flip you off while you were establishing eye-to-eye contact with them. "I love it when they give me the middle finger because I just wave to them and smile! This always embarrasses Wild Dogs and is the first step in their taming and training process. In most cases, their middle finger drops and they wave back with an embarrassed look on

229

their face because they realize we were just trying to be friendly to them.

"Okay, get ready; here we come, wave everybody!" This particular Wild Dog must have been having a very bad day and was probably in a big hurry to get back to his lair and feed his offspring because he flipped us off while we were waving and continued to do so as we passed by him. As a matter of fact, based on his facial expression, I think he dropped the F-bomb on us also!

"He flipped us off!" exclaimed Mark, while all of the trainees started laughing. "Of course he did Mark. That is very normal, but the possible F-bomb was not! Okay, Mark, make sure you shadow your brake and look left, right, left, right before we enter the next watering hole. The next watering hole is called Leonard Street, and after that is Knapp, and then Three Mile. Our goal is to make it all the way to the Grand River without having to stop at any of the traffic lights.

"Knapp is about a mile up the trail. Here he comes again. He's cutting back and forth between the other animals with no signal in sight! There he goes, right by us! Okay, watch as he approaches the light at Knapp. See, he's braking at the last minute again. Here we go; the light's green! Wave as we go by him. Look at that! He double flipped us off and definitely dropped the F-bomb on us! He is a very angry Wild Dog."

Even though our windows were rolled up, the laughter was so loud, I was sure every other animal on the road could hear us. Mark was concerned that our training

efforts weren't going to work and said, "He's not getting the message. All we are doing is making him angrier!" I told Mark, "Don't worry Mark. We have to be patient with him. Remember, A Wild Dog is a very difficult animal to tame."

The next series of events were almost mystical, and maybe with a little help from divine intervention, our taming and training efforts paid off. As we approached the next watering hole, the Wild Dog in the Porsche roared by us again. But, this time the outcome was vastly different. It was almost as if the sky above us parted and a beam of light from the heavens shined down upon the Wild Dog and the Beast!

He began to slow down until we caught up to him, so now we were driving side by side. We looked over to him, and he at us, but this time he took his four fingers and saluted us with a smile and then, instead of flipping us off, he gave us an "okay" gesture with his fingers. Neither of us had to stop at the light because it had turned green. We both proceeded through the watering hole with the wonderful green light, and as we both sailed off into the sunset, he waved and saluted to us again as if to make sure we knew he was grateful to us for showing him the error of his ways. Our safari was successful, our taming and training session was complete, and we tamed a Wild Dog! It was a glorious moment in the Jungle!

This, however, is not the end of our story. A couple of months later at the conclusion of one of my parent training sessions, I shared this story with the parents. I noticed a parent in the back of the room laughing hysterically throughout the entire story. Although the story is rather amusing, this parent was laughing much more than the rest of the audience. When the training session ended, the same parent came up to me and, still laughing, shared with me the fact that he knew the guy in the story. He told me that he was a financial planner and the Wild Dog in the story was one of his clients. He knew the story was true because during one of their financial planning meetings, the Wild Dog shared the story with him and it was exactly as I told it. We both had another good laugh.

Guess what? I'm not finished yet. The story continues! About a couple of months after the rush hour safari, I was in the Beast and on the road again with another group of Jungle students. We were at an intersection waiting at a red light. We were in the left lane and we were going to proceed straight through the intersection. To our left was a left turn lane. As part of *The Jungle Way*, I was explaining to the driver that while waiting at the red light, we never want to stare at the lights of the animal in front of us. When you stare at anything for too long, it becomes an eye-holding problem and then we fixate on it. Once this happens we become like a Lemming. Once the light turns green, we just start following the other

Lemmings through the intersection without looking, and off the cliff to

our death.

I was telling the young driver to look at the animals around us because they usually provide us with a lot of free entertainment with the things they do inside their vehicles. At this point, the light turned green. Jungle drivers all know that a green light means death, and in order to stop from dying we have to protect the weakest part of the car, the side, by looking and seeing left, right, left, right, and checking what's coming up behind us before proceeding. At that exact moment, in the left lane, we noticed a black Porsche Cayenne Turbo traveling at a high rate of speed coming up very fast to the intersection. I placed my foot on my secondary brake and instructed my student not to move. The animal behind us began to beep their horn because we were not moving through the intersection. Whoosh! The Porsche blew by us from the left lane into our lane just barely avoiding the oncoming traffic and raced up the road traveling at least 55 mph in a 25 mph zone! The young driver immediately screamed, "Hey, that's the Wild Dog you told us about!" I said, "It sure is!" The young driver enthusiastically responded with, "Let's catch him!" We all laughed hysterically.

This was another good lesson learned in the Jungle about what not to do. I continually teach my students that sometimes, the most difficult part of driving *The Jungle Way* is that Jungle drivers drive the opposite of everyone else in the Jungle. That is why it is so important that we teach their parents *The Jungle Way* so parents can be the true driving role models for their teenagers.

Even bad drivers on the road can be a learning point for teen drivers.

# Chapter 20

## Epilogue

So that's the Jungle story, and this would be a great time to end this book, but there is one very important concept we have left to discuss. At Jungle Survival Drivers Training we often talk about the process of learning to drive as one of the few "rites of passage" available to young adults in our culture. What we also do is provide them a vehicular doorway to the widening world of adulthood – the automobile. It's an important step in their education. We send them off on the roadways, and pray and hope for their safety and good decision making, relying on their learned skills.

Jungle Survival Drivers Training begins with several underlying principles that are in the background of everything we do. It has become, in many ways, what we preach, and how we do business all in one. It is what we believe in, and try to instill in every one of our students.

Not only should we give this rite of passage proper respect and attention as we have done throughout this book, and each and every day of the week, 365 days a year at Jungle Survival Drivers Training, but we should also make sure this doorway leads somewhere decent, responsible, and capable of improving the quality of life here on our evermore complex planet. I know that doesn't sound much like the highways and byways you and I encounter on our daily grind through traffic. In fact, most times it's anything but. Yet herein lays the potential of driving to be something more than just a means to get from point A to point B, or even to get there in a safety-conscious, highly proficient, "Jungle" kind of way. You see, driving is a common ground on which members of our human tribe meet and exchange connection and communication. If we take the time to pay attention to those communications and the actions we choose while driving, we can move ourselves and our fellow travelers a little further each day toward a more supportive, positive, and caring social culture. Courteous driving should be our habit. Safety should be our priority. And we all (parents and teens) should practice this creed every day.

We teach courtesy, decency, and safety to our drivers at Jungle. We teach respect, situational driving, and a skill-set that is practical. Although it might seem to be "theoretical," *The Jungle Way* is not. It is proven with facts and statistics to improve driver safety and survivability. That is why our program is very different. How we apply it on the road is what matters.

When I got serious about writing this book, my co-writer asked me to answer three simple questions about the book I wanted to write. After re-reading those answers in my notes, I have concluded that those answers provide a good summary and conclusion to my business and our corporate goals at Jungle. It is what I believe, and how I have tried to carry this message forward to the teenage drivers of our generation. It has become my philosophy, my creed, to devote myself to the safety of teen drivers.

First, he asked me to describe the book in one simple sentence, as it might appear in *The New York Times* "Book Review List" in the Sunday newspaper. I answered this – "*The Jungle Way* is the most effective driver training solution ever designed for parents who want to keep their teenager safe and alive whether they are behind the wheel or a passenger in a motor vehicle."

Secondly, he asked me to tell him what I would say if someone on the street, a neighbor, a friend, a relative that you meet one day hears about your book and asks for you to briefly describe it in two to three sentences. I told him, "I wrote this book because I care. I am gravely concerned about the number of teenagers who are dying on our nation's roads. These deaths don't need to happen, and we need to do something about it. Within the pages of my book are the solutions to keeping teenagers safe and alive behind the wheel."

Finally, he asked me to write down and define the objective of the book, as in a short mission statement for the project. He asked me to tell him what I wished to achieve in this book. I wrote, "The objective of this book is to motivate, inspire, instruct, and educate teens and parents so they can work together learning how to survive in the highway Jungle."

I believe I have done that with this book – it is everything that I am about.

It is my hope that this book summarizes the Jungle Survival Drivers Training program in a manner which helps teenagers and parents in many practical ways. It is my prayer and hope that it saves more lives and increases driving safety for teenagers taking to the road. If it saves even one teenager's life someday in the future and prevents a family tragedy, it will all have been worthwhile.

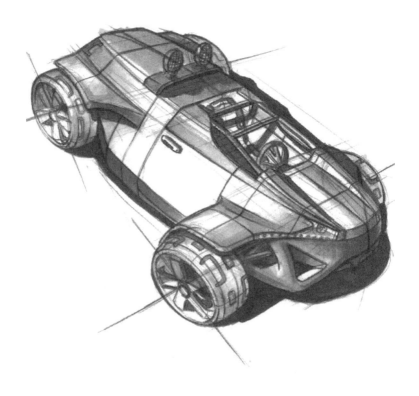

# Chapter 21

## The Jungle Way Survival Methods

1.     WHEN STOPPED BEHIND ANOTHER ANIMAL AT A WATERING HOLE, MAKE SURE YOU HAVE (1) JUNGLE WAY CAR LENGTH OF SPACE (a Jungle Way car length is about one and a half car lengths)

•      This helps you to not get trapped behind another animal that is disabled at the watering hole because you will have enough room to move around them.

•      If another animal bumps you from behind there is less of a chance you could get knocked into the animal ahead of you.

•      When the jungle paths are slippery due to snow or rain and the animal approaching you from behind loses its footing, this extra space may prevent a rear end collision. You can move forward to allow the out of control animal a little more stopping distance behind you.

•      The best way to create your Jungle Way car length is by doing the following: As you are approaching the stopped animal in front of you, look underneath it at its front tires and come to a complete stop just before its tires disappear from your view. Remember to check your mirrors before applying your brakes!

•      The Jungle Way car length is the first step in re-establishing your proper following distance (4-6 seconds under 30 mph and 6-8 seconds over 30mph) after moving away from the watering hole.

• Establishing this space keeps you far enough away from the animals in front of you so you will be able to GET THE BIG PICTURE while LEAVING YOURSELF AN OUT.

2.   BEFORE MAKING THE DECISION TO CROSS THROUGH THE WATERING HOLE MAKE SURE TO LOOK AND SEE LEFT-RIGHT-LEFT (2) AND RIGHT AGAIN

•      All Jungle drivers know that a green light does NOT mean go! It means death. A green light is telling you to look and see left-right-left-right to determine if it is safe to proceed across the watering hole.

•      The side of an animal is its weakest point; don't make the fatal mistake of not looking left, right, left, and right before moving.

•      Remember: Over 40% of all fatal accidents occur at watering holes (17,000 people are killed at watering holes each year and 10,000 of those are due to side impact attacks).

•      Looking and seeing Left-Right-Left-Right is essential to staying alive at watering holes and KEEPING YOUR EYES MOVING.

3.   WHEN STOPPED AT A WATERING HOLE BEHIND ANOTHER ANIMAL, COUNT TO (3) AFTER THE ANIMAL IN FRONT OF YOU HAS STARTED TO MOVE

•      Doing so will automatically help you re-establish the proper following distance of 4 to 6 and 6 to 8 seconds.

•      Use this method while first checking your mirrors and then looking Left-Right-Left-Right.

•       Remember – The first 4 seconds (The Fatal Four) after the light turns green is the most likely time you will be struck by a stampeding wild animal.

•       Counting 1 – 2 – 3 buys time, allowing you to GET THE BIG PICTURE.

4.      ONE OF THE THREE AREAS OF SPACE YOU CAN CONTROL IS FRONT OF YOU. MAKE SURE TO ESTABLISH A (4) TO 6 SECOND FOLLOWING DISTANCE BETWEEN YOU AND THE ANIMAL IN FRONT OF YOU FOR SPEEDS UNDER 30 MPH AND 6 TO 8 SECONDS FOR SPEEDS OVER 30 MPH

•       This prevents you from staring at the rear end of the animal in front of you.  Brake based on what you see not the animal you are following.

•       Doing so allows you to establish and maintain the proper eye lead-time (the number of seconds you are looking down the road in front of you), which helps you AIM HIGH IN STEERING.

•       You won't become a "Butt Sniffer" (Tail Gating) if you maintain these following distances.

•       Maintaining this following distance buys you time so you can anticipate mistakes other animals might make in front of you, ensuring that you LEAVE YOURSELF AN OUT.

•       By staying back and seeing it all, you are able to GET THE BIG PICTURE.

5.    LOOK BEHIND AND TO THE SIDES OF YOU FOR OTHER ANIMALS, AT LEAST, EVERY (5) TO 8 SECONDS

•    Doing so contributes to your awareness of what surrounds you in the jungle.

•    Make sure to check mirrors: before braking, before & after a turn, before & after a path change, before & after a watering hole, before & after passing another animal, when you pass an ant waiting to cross a street, and when an Gator is waiting to pull out in front of you.

•    Don't forget to use the Jungle Way mirror setting to eliminate your blind spots.  Remember – blind spots are not caused by the design of the animal, but by improper adjustment of the mirrors.

•    Scanning, and not staring, ensures that you KEEP YOUR EYES MOVING.

6.    SCAN FOR GATORS - Scan and six begin with an S.

•    Scan steering wheels of animals parked alongside the path, in driveways, and in swamps (parking lots).

•    By doing so, you can see whether someone is behind the wheel of the animal, helping you identify "Gators."

•    If a Gator is occupied, the driver is probably about to get out, pull from the path's edge, or back out of a driveway or mud hole (parking space).

•      Make sure to look for back up lights, brake lights, exhaust fumes, doors opening or wheels turning from the edge of the path.

•      By scanning steering wheels of Gators, you can identify doubtful situations by KEEPING YOUR EYES MOVING.

7.      STALE GREEN LIGHTS - (7) starts with an S and so does stale.

•      A Stale Green Light is a light at the watering hole that you didn't see turn green, so you are unsure of when it will turn red.

•      You must first determine your Point of Decision (POD). Your POD is an imaginary line that you establish between yourself and the watering hole.

•      Option A: If you do not reach your POD before the light turns yellow, you must apply the brake and stop when you can see the stop line in front of you just beyond the edge of the hood (about ½ an animal's length back from the line).

•      Option B: If you do reach your POD before the light turns yellow, proceed across the watering hole while shadowing the brake and looking Left, Right, Left, Right and checking your mirrors.

•   You can Identify Stale Green Lights by AIMING HIGH IN STEERING and GETTING THE BIG PICTURE.

8.   SEARCH THE PATH IN FRONT OF YOU AT LEAST (8) TO 12 SECONDS FOR DOUBTFUL SITUATIONS

•   By looking 8 to 12 seconds or as far as you can see down the path, you can plan ahead to avoid surprises.

•   AIMING HIGH IN STEERING centers you on the path, as well as providing a safe path on turns.

•   By identifying doubtful situations well ahead, you won't be taken by surprise by the mistakes other animals make.

•   By staying back and seeing it all, you GET THE BIG PICTURE, and can be proactive as to what might happen further up the path.

9.   WHEN PULLING FROM THE PATH'S EDGE OR CHANGING A PATH, REMEMBER TO SMMS (Signal, Mirror, Mirror, Shoulder). Looking over the shoulder forms the number (9).

•   Performing this check confirms what you have been seeing while checking your mirrors regularly (#5).

•   Don't always trust your mirrors, they only show a small part of the Big Picture, use your eyes as much as possible!

•     By scanning, not staring, you KEEP YOUR EYES MOVING, preventing sideswipes, close calls and collisions.

10.   ESTABLISH EYE CONTACT WITH THE OTHER ANIMALS - Eye Contact has (10) letters.

•     When depending on other animals to maintain their course, it is essential to get their attention.

•     The horn, lights and signals are your communication tools when you do not have eye contact. Use the horn before and not after an animal makes a mistake!

•     By establishing eye- to - eye contact with other animals you avoid being taken by surprise.

•     Establishing Eye Contact is the best way to MAKE SURE THEY SEE YOU.

The 5 Rules of Space & Visibility Driving

How do you do it? What does it do for you? Key phrase –
REMEMBER…

1. **AIM HIGH IN STEERING**

Imaginary target – baseball/dartboard.

Centers your car in traffic lane: Safe path on turns.

"FIND A SAFE PATH WELL AHEAD."

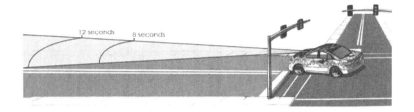

## 2. GET THE BIG PICTURE

How wide and deep? What's in it? Objects and background.

Keeps you away from billboards. Smooth stops and turns.

Buys time.

"STAY BACK AND SEE IT ALL."


## 3. KEEP YOUR EYES MOVING

Move eyes: Front – 2 seconds. Rear – 5 to 8 seconds.

Keeps you alive at intersections. Keeps eyes ahead of car.

"SCAN – DON'T STARE."


## 4. LEAVE YOURSELF AN OUT

Have an escape route. Take path of least resistance.

Space on all four sides, but always in front.

"BE PREPARED. EXPECT THE UNEXPECTED."

## 5. MAKE SURE THEY SEE YOU

Communicate in traffic – horn, lights, and signals.

Establishes eye-to-eye contact.

"DON'T GAMBLE. USE YOUR HORN, LIGHTS AND SIGNALS."

Tip for Memorization - **All = Aim    Good = Get    Kids = Keep    Like = Leave    Milk = Make**

THE END

For general information on our program, including franchise opportunities, please contact our corporate office headquarters:

JUNGLE SURVIVAL DRIVERS TRAINING, Inc.

6090 East Fulton Street

Suite C

Ada, Michigan

49301

Telephone # 616-676-4600

FAX # 616-676-4606

Email: Jungle1950@comcast.net

Visit Our Website at: www.junglejsdt.com

Find us on FACEBOOK by searching for

RaRa JuMa

or

Jungle Survival Drivers Training

# Author's Notes

## Mark A. Werkema

When I was asked to help write this book with Randy Rand, I scarcely realized the journey and education which would follow in the process. It was indeed a learning experience – one which I as a parent needed to experience to help convey the importance of the subject matter.

I was a parent who put two teen daughters through The Jungle program – and I am very thankful I did. I believe in this program, and what it teaches teen drivers on many levels – the practical education aspects of driving, but more importantly the attitude and mindset which Randy Rand instills in his students who learn to drive The Jungle Way. It is truly a unique program that saves teen lives – that is why I wanted to help tell his story and communicate his philosophy in this book.

Parents, this book and The Jungle Program are precious gifts you can give your teen driver which will affect their lives forever.

Students, this book and The Jungle Program is a unique program which, you may or may not understand fully now, but *will* save your life someday, and help you on the journey on the road wherever you travel in life.

Teen driving safety is a topic of great importance that demands more attention in our nation, and around the world. When we were writing this book, one day I came across a USA TODAY newspaper article on the front page entitled "Parents May Be the Key to Driver's Ed" which related the importance of proper and focused teen driving education and parental involvement (a topic which Jungle highly promotes and encourages). The statistics are daunting, and humbling in many respects. That is one reason I decided to help with this book project – Randy Rand, a friend and admirable man of great passion and expertise had developed a teen driving program that had a distinct and different message, and he needed to get his message out and his story told. This book is the result of our work.

Every parent is concerned and worried about their child who takes to the road. This book details the program that *can* and *will* help a parent deal with the stress that goes with the territory every time their teen driver backs out of the driveway on to the road. We all know the fear, the concern, and the worry – we want our teens to be safe. This program aids us as parents in dealing with that overriding concern for our children.

As a parent, I appreciated his corporate motto and his genuine concern for teen drivers. His goal and objective was clear and distinct – help save teenage drivers' lives. That's really what he is all about, and has devoted his company and mission statement to promote road safety and driving skills in teenagers that are first learning to drive. What he has developed in his clearly unique business model is a program that is effective and works, as well as one that has a lasting impression on the teens that learn in the program, and apply it to the road every time they head out into the Jungle.

When we embarked on this project I was a naïve parent, one that had heard of his program, but in truth, was not fully aware of its uniqueness, powerful concepts, and principles. I quickly learned – this was a very different company, and a very different program. I am a writer, but I am also a parent who put two daughters through the Jungle Survival Drivers Training program and benefited from the safety and skill set which was instilled in my children by taking his course. It was money well spent, and in truth, I would have paid much more for the experience that my two daughters gained and the education they received.

*The Jungle Way* is a must-read for every teenager driver out there – its benefits are immense. It is also a must-read for any parent of a teen driver. As a father, I speak to fellow parents, and ask you to let this book help your teenager, as it did mine.

I believe that this book details the four primary tenets of the Jungle program. Above all else, it is first a proven, effective way to teach your teenager to drive safely. Second, it increases safety through training. Third, it encourages parent involvement to maximize benefits and creates a partnership of safety. And finally, it instills life-long safe driving skills that are learned as a teenager.

This I know: *The Jungle Way* works and the results are amazing. This book is an inspiration to students and parents – and hopefully increases safety in the process.

It has been said that the training and mindset approach that Jungle has instituted in their curriculum is a gift that the teens can take with them for the rest of their lives – how true. It has been my privilege and distinct honor to help tell the story of a dedicated and thoughtful man who has devoted his life to saving teen lives on the road, and grown a company which developed into a unique icon of hope that has become an example of how to properly train safe teen drivers, and give them those foundational skills to carry with them forever in their daily lives ahead when they take to the road.

Parents and students – thank you for reading this book and applying The Jungle Way program, it is a valuable resource which will save teen drivers lives.

Mark A. Werkema

Writer

East Grand Rapids, Michigan

# Appendices

## THE JUNGLE WAY ENHANCED MIRROR ADJUSTMENT

1- Proper adjustment of the mirrors is key to situational awareness within the car. Here, I am standing where the driver's blind spot is located.

2- While sitting in the driver's seat, move the mirror adjustment switch to the left mirror.

3- Lean to your left and place your left cheek against the driver's side window and move the mirror out so the left back corner of the vehicle is visible.

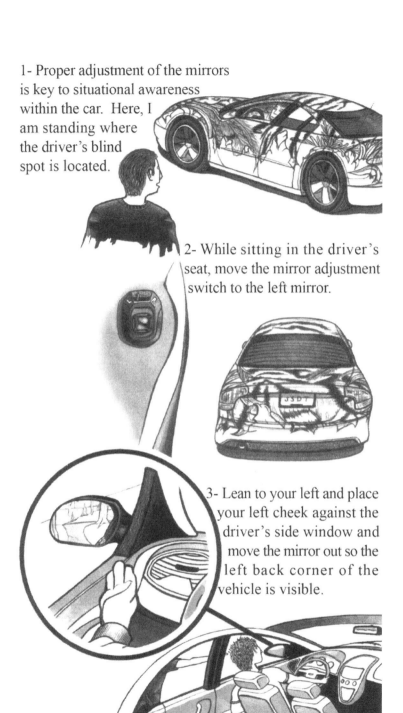

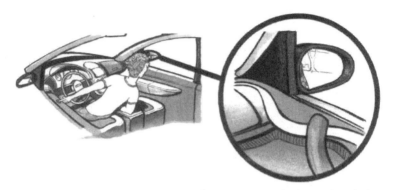

4- After moving the mirror adjustment switch to the right mirror, lean to the right past mid-center of the car and move the right mirror all the way out until just the right rear corner is visible.

5- Adjust the rear view mirror so you can see the entire rear window without moving your head.

6- After these simple adjustments, you now have eliminated your blind spots in your mirrors.

7- The series of illustrations demonstrate the effectiveness of properly adjusted mirrors in determining the movement of cars around you within the area that, prior to your adjustment, would have contained a blind spot.

8- The person standing behind the car is a demonstration of another vehicle passing on the left side of your vehicle.

9- Now, the person represents the car next to your vehicle as it passes you on the left side.

10- This position is a car approaching from the rear and passing on the right.

11- As the car moves along your side, you can still see it in your right side mirror.

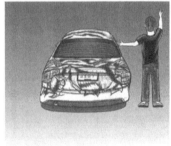

12- Now, while driving you will be in a position to never lose contact with the cars around you in what was previously the blind spot areas. If your mirrors are properly adjusted, you should never lose visual contact with the vehicle.

# ARE YOU READY FOR THE JUNGLE TEST?

Questions:

1)    A skilled driver makes _____ (number of) mistakes per driving hour?

2)    When do the majority of intersection accidents occur?

3)    What type of roads are the most dangerous: urban, suburban, commercial, rural, or highway?

4)    If you are the first car in line to turn left at an intersection you can turn when _____

5)    Following distance should be equal to one car length for every 10 mph. True___ False___

6)    What percentage of drivers are under the influence of alcohol between 4:30 and 8:30 P.M.?    1%   5%   10% 20%  30%  40%

7)    Approximately how many feet can a vehicle moving at 30 mph travel before the driver can apply the brake?

8)    What behavior can decrease your chances of an accident in a parking lot by at least 33%?

9) The best way to reduce point-to-point driving time is by: (a) increasing speed, (b) coasting up to vehicles waiting at a light, (c) taking roads that are more familiar.

10) Due to aspects of their brain development men are generally better drivers than women. True___ False___

11) In order to make a safe and legal lane change you must signal at least _____ blinks prior to the lane change.

12) A vehicle striking a fixed object at 35 mph is the equivalent of approximately _____ times the force of gravity?

13) What is the first thing to do if your dashboard gauge indicates your engine is overheating?

14) Lane changes in intersections are discouraged, but not illegal. True___ False___

Answers:

1)    [Mistakes per hour] A skilled driver makes 30 driving decisions every minute and for every 500 decisions they make one mistake. That equates to almost four mistakes for every hour they drive.

2)    [Traffic light accidents] The first four seconds after a traffic light changes from red to green is when the majority of intersection accidents occur.

3)    [The most dangerous roads] and least often trained for are rural or country roads where high speeds, two-lane passing driveways and side streets combine to create major hazards.

4)    [You can turn when] You must move forward into the intersection, stop when your rear tires are passed the pedestrian crosswalk and keep your front wheels straight. Once you have legally established your position in the intersection you can complete your turn on red if the traffic doesn't clear on the green light. If any part of your car is resting on the crosswalk and you turn on red, then you are running the red light.

5)    [Following distance] False. This method doesn't take into consideration reaction time, stopping distance, feet per second traveled and swerving space. You must establish and maintain a four to six second following distance under 30 mph and a six to eight second following distance for speeds over 30 mph. (This should be adjusted up when there is a change in traction due to weather.)

6)     [Percentage under the influence] Between the hours of 4:30 and 8:30 P.M., one out of ten drivers are under the influence of alcohol and after 11:00 P.M. over 50% of all traffic accidents are alcohol related.

7)     [How many feet] Reaction time for a good driver is 1 ½ seconds from the time you recognize a problem and you remove your foot from the accelerator and apply the brake.  At 30 mph this means you have traveled <u>over 65 feet</u> before you even apply the brake.  (This is the equivalent to about five car lengths.)

8)     [Parking lot accidents] Pulling through a parking space, or backing into it, will reduce your chances of an accident by 33% and a new driver's by 50%!

9)     [Point-to-point time] Ultimately it will <u>cost</u> you time by speeding and taking chances, and familiarity does not change speed limits, lights or signs. The fastest way to get from point A to point B is to look far enough ahead to coast up to vehicles that are waiting at the light and not have to stop your vehicle.  If you don't have to stop your vehicle while driving you will average a higher rate of speed and will get to your location sooner (and much safer).

10)    [Men and women] In actuality, men have accidents over three times the rate of women.  Men get stopped and ticketed more than three times the rate of women.  Men get stopped for driving under the influence over three times the rate of women.

11)    [Turn signal use] At least four blinks of the signal and after the last street before your intended turn.

12)    [Striking an object at 35 mph] The equivalent of 50 times the force of gravity. This is five times more than the astronauts have to withstand when they take off in the space shuttle. Ouch!

13)    [Overheating] If your vehicle is overheating, turning the cabin heater on high with the windows open may disperse the heat. If this does not work, stopping the vehicle is the next option.

14)    [Lane changes] False. It is illegal to change lanes in an intersection or when driving over railroad tracks.

The 5 Rules of Space & Visibility Driving


## Practical Facts That Can Save Your Life


1. A skilled driver makes thirty driving decisions every minute, and for every 500 decisions they make one mistake. That equates to almost four mistakes for every hour they drive.

2. The first four seconds after a traffic light changes from red to green is when the majority of intersection accidents occur. Remember that a green light doesn't mean go; it means it is safe to look and see left, right, left, and right. People die at green lights, not red. The side of the car is the weakest part and must be protected. Of the 40,000 people killed every year in auto accidents, 17,000 happen at

intersections, and 10,000 of those are side-impact collisions.

3.  When making a left turn at a green light and you are the first car in traffic and there is oncoming traffic, you must move forward into the intersection and stop when your rear tires are past the pedestrian crosswalk and keep your front wheels straight. This is important so if you are struck in the rear, you will not be pushed at an angle into oncoming traffic. It is also important that the traffic signal is still visible. Once you have legally established your position in the intersection, you can complete your turn on red if the traffic doesn't clear on the green light. If any part of your car is resting on the crosswalk and you turn on red, you are running the red light.

4.  You learned when you were younger that you must maintain a following distance equal to one car length for every 10 mph. This is incorrect because it doesn't take into consideration reaction time, stopping distance, feet per second traveled, and swerving space. We teach our students to establish and maintain a four to six second following distance under 30 mph, and a six to eight second following distance for speeds over 30 mph. This should be adjusted up when there is a change in traction due to weather.

5.  Between the hours of 4:30 and 8:30 P.M., one out of ten drivers are under the influence of alcohol. After 11:00 P.M., over 50% of all traffic accidents are alcohol related.

6.  Reaction time for a good driver is 1 ½ seconds from the time you recognize a problem and you remove your foot

from the accelerator and apply the brake. At 30 mph this means you have traveled over 65 feet before you even apply the brake. This is equivalent to about five car lengths.

7. The difference between defensive driving and situational driving is when you are using defensive driving skills, you identify a problem on the road and react to the problem by braking or swerving to avoid a collision. Depending on your level of awareness you might recognize the problem soon enough to take the appropriate action and the result is usually referred to as a close call. Situational driving is more of a proactive approach to driving. It requires the driver of the car to be much more attentive and involved in the actual driving process. Instead of identifying a problem and then reacting, situational driving skills allow you to identify a situation before it develops into a problem. This allows a driver to make a proactive response and adjustments are made much sooner, so the result is much more planned and expected. Think of it as making the unexpected the expected.

8. There are three beliefs that people should never argue about: religion, politics, and how they drive a car. Nothing positive ever results from these discussions.

9. One-third of all adults and one-half of all teen accidents come as a result of backing up. Even the addition of

cameras and beepers doesn't appear to have reduced the number of these accidents. Learn to pull through into a parking space to position your vehicle in the direction you will be going next. If you are unable to pull through, back into the space you are parking in.

10. You cannot make time in traffic by speeding and taking chances. The best way to get from point A to point B is to drive less aggressively by backing off traffic lights much sooner and learning to coast up to vehicles that are waiting at the light. If you don't have to stop your vehicle while driving, you will average a higher rate of speed and will get to your location sooner and much safer, without breaking the law. Remember the tortoise won the race with the hare.

11. Men have accidents at 3.64 times the rate of women. Men get stopped and ticketed more than three times the rate of women. Men get stopped for driving under the influence over three times the rate of women. This comes from a study performed in 2008 by Quality Planning, Inc. for the insurance industry. The study included over one million drivers equally divided between men and women. It's true: women are better drivers than men.

12. In order to make a safe and legal lane change, you must signal for at least four blinks prior to the lane change. You then must check the rear view mirror, and when you can see the headlights of the vehicle behind you, check the outside mirror on the side you are moving to, and then make a visual check over the shoulder out the rear door window. You must complete this check over the shoulder without moving the shoulders or steering wheel.

13.     A vehicle striking a fixed object at 30 mph is the equivalent of 50 times the force of gravity. That is five times more than astronauts have to withstand when they take off in a space shuttle. This means that everything inside the car is moving with the same force. This is why it is so important to place all loose items in your trunk and make sure everyone is wearing their seat belts. A 150-pound unbelted person or a school book bag is a lethal weapon that is flying around inside a vehicle striking a fixed object.

14.     Inexperienced teenage drivers should not drive a vehicle unless it has front and side airbags.

15.     Auto accidents are the leading killer of teenagers in the United Stated. Out of all teenagers who die in this country, 36% do so as a result of an auto accident. In the first one to three years of driving, 80% of teenagers will have some sort of auto accident. Almost 15% of teenage drivers will experience a serious accident during their first twelve months of unsupervised driving. Less than 10% of Jungle drivers will have an accident during their first one to three years of driving.

16.     Never beep your horn after someone makes a mistake. Use your horn in a friendly manner prior to the mistake to alert them of your presence. Do this while shadowing your brake until you make eye contact with the other person.

17.     The only way you can be sure you have made a complete stop at a stop sign or a right turn on red is when you experience a slight bounce back after applying the

brakes. Remember that 75% of all accidents take place at an average speed of 19 mph.

18.    Every driver of a vehicle thought they were a good driver before they were killed in an auto accident.

19.    Drive in direct proportion to the loss of traction in inclement weather. This means to never let the wheels of your vehicle spin or slide when you are stopping or starting. Spinning wheels are telling you that you are driving too fast for conditions and to slow down and get off the gas. Remember, a spinning wheel is a split second before a sliding wheel. Use the tachometer as an early warning system for a spinning wheel. When you are driving during inclement weather, keep an eye on the tachometer. If the needle spikes to indicate a sudden increase in RPMs, this means your vehicle is about to go into a skid. Immediately get off the gas without applying the brakes. Then drive at a speed where the tachometer holds steady for the speed you are traveling. This would be a safe speed for the conditions.

20.    Don't ignore your tires. Proper tread depth and properly inflated tires are vital for the safety of everyone on the road. Make sure to evaluate the tread depth by using the wear bars that manufacturers design into the tread. When the wear bars are visible toward the surface of the tire, replace the tire.